Himalayan Tragedy

The story of Tibet's Panchen Lamas

by

David White

David White has travelled widely throughout the Himalayas. He is a Fellow of the Royal Geographical Society. This is his first book.

Cover design by Goosey Graphics Company, Shrewsbury.

© David White

First published 2002
by The Tibet Society of the UK
Unit 9
139 Fonthill Road
London N4 3HF

Printed and bound in Great Britain by Bell & Bain Ltd, Scotland

0-9542179-0-X

This book is dedicated to
Gedhun Choekyi Nyima

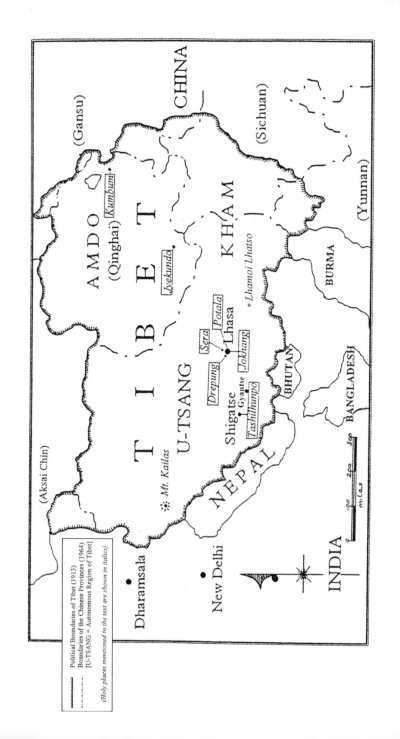

Contents

Acknowledgements

My thanks go to the Royal College of Defence Studies, which provided the opportunity for research, Zara Fleming whose chairmanship of the Tibet Society inspired my interest, Philippa Carrick who formatted the text, Ian Cumming of Tibet Images who provided the photographs, and Dr. Tim Mitford who so patiently struggled with my early drafts.

List of Illustrations

Photos are reprinted by kind permission of Tibet Images, London. Web: www.tibetimages.co.uk; Telephone 020 7278 2377 Hugh Richardson by kind permission of Roger Croston.

Foreword

The present Dalai Lama, Tenzin Gyatso, is renowned throughout the world, and his Government in Exile at Dharamsala has kept the West informed of the general situation in Tibet. Less is known about Tibet's second most important religious office, the Panchen Lama. Its holders have been controversial figures who continue to influence history today. My purpose is to explain the origins of the lineage and its impact upon modern politics.

The name for Tibet, *Gangs-ljongs* (Land of Snows), which inaccurately describes the climate, alerts the researcher to its inherent contradictions. While it is indeed a spiritual place of magical beauty, the perception that its inhabitants are a gentle, unsophisticated race who have been exploited for their political naivety is mistaken. The foundation of Tibet's religious leadership, its status as a nation and China's claim upon it, are intricate.

Fearing interference in their spiritual heritage, Tibetans are wary of foreigners. Yet they have courted relationships with the Mongolian, British, Russian and Chinese empires at different times throughout their long history. This is a story of labyrinthine complexity, intertwined with the manipulations of a powerful religious hierarchy, which is fraught with medieval intrigue.

Tibet's past record of international diplomacy and politics is important for understanding the position today, but the brevity of this account precludes an in-depth analysis of all its history. Similarly, the treatment of Tibetans by China during the Cultural Revolution (1966-1976), which must rank in brutality alongside Stalin's Purges and the Nazi Holocaust, cannot receive the full attention it deserves.

I have therefore focused upon the relationship between the two leading religious dynasties, the Dalai and Panchen Lamas, which are known to Tibetans as 'the Sun and the Moon', and upon the significance of China's behaviour towards them, including the selection of the latest *tulku* (reincarnation of a lama). The historical background, prior to 1900, will be confined to the key events that explain the lamas' rise to power and Tibet's relationship with neighbouring empires. Recent events, particularly those that concerned British involvement, will be covered in more detail.

With this short publication, I hope to provide a brief insight into the mysteries of this wonderful yet tragic land and stimulate further interest.

Tibetan names, which are shown in italics, are explained in the glossary.

David White
London, 2002

Introduction

After crossing into Tibet from the Nepalese border at Zhangmu, the rugged road to the capital, Lhasa ('place of the Gods'), climbs steeply and precariously through the Himalayas to the first great pass at Lalung *la*, 16,500 feet above sea level. The landscape that unfolds in the Tingri plateau beyond is like no other on earth. With no trees at this altitude, only the small golden barley fields, cultivated for the Tibetan staple diet of *tsampa*, and brilliant turquoise rivers provide colour on the barren ground beneath the mountain ranges. The crisp light in this thin air gives the place an eerie, yet wondrous, quality.

A sense of the Tibetans' deep spiritual faith is evident throughout this rural region. The passes are littered with small prayer flags, and, in the villages, the identical single storey houses are similarly adorned, their whitewashed walls painted with coloured stripes according to the religious sect of their owners. Even the yaks carry charms for good fortune.

In technological terms, time appears to have stood still since the Middle Ages. The wheel, which abundant in a religious context, is a relatively recent innovation as a means of transport. But, despite obvious poverty and widespread illiteracy, the charming and

Introduction

unfailingly friendly country folk, with their fancifully decorated pigtails, smiling Mongoloid faces and colourful clothes do not seem unhappy.

However, a more sinister dimension soon mars this impression of an idyllic land. Near every intact homestead lie the ruins of once great buildings as barely concealed witnesses to recent violence and misery. Aggressive People's Liberation Army (PLA) guards at the prefecture boundaries remind the traveller that this is not a free country and, in the towns, Chinese influence abounds.

After nearly 400 miles on the slow and hazardous journey to Lhasa, civilisation is reached for the first time at Shigatse, the second largest city in Tibet. A short distance from this austere town of 1950s Communist architecture lies the splendid monastery of Tashilhunpo. This extensive community consists of a maze of mystical buildings with striking golden roofs, a great *thangka* wall for displaying huge icons, and strange white *stupas* that contain the sacred relics of former hierarchs. Founded by the First Dalai Lama, Gendun Drub, in 1447, it has nevertheless been the seat of the Panchen Lamas since the 17th century.

However, there is little evidence of the 4,000 monks who lived here before the Cultural Revolution, and those few encountered appear subdued. Only the monastery dogs appear in abundance; reputedly the reincarnations of less pious inhabitants. Pilgrims shuffle silently past carrying their prayer wheels and little pots of yak butter, to prostrate themselves before the immense statue of *Maitreya*, and offer their white silk *Khata* with solemn, unsmiling devotion. The reason for this lack of gaiety, uncharacteristic of the Tibetan people, is that Tashilhunpo has become the focus for political manipulation of their faith.

Inside the ancient Dukhang Assembly Hall, behind the Panchen Lama's throne and the main altar, there is a small chapel called the Drolma *Lhakhang*. Here, amidst the dark pungent atmosphere of flickering yak-butter lamps, can be found the faded photograph of an intelligent-looking six-year-old boy whose name is Gedhun Choekyi Nyima. He is recognised by Tibetans as the reincarnated 11th Panchen Lama. A few days after his appointment was announced in May 1995, the Chinese abducted the boy and his family. They have never been seen since.

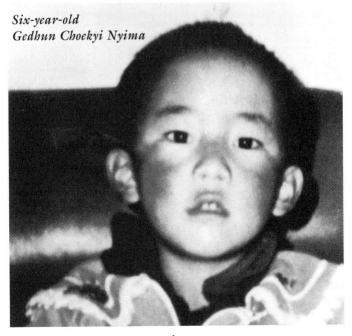

Six-year-old
Gedhun Choekyi Nyima

1

Tibet's religious and political origins

Early history

According to Tibetan annals, the first king of Tibet ruled from 127 BC, but it was only in the 7th century AD that Tibet emerged as a unified state under Emperor Songtsen Gampo. This legendary king acceded to the throne when he was thirteen and reigned for many years. His armies captured Upper Burma and the provinces of Kansu, Szechuan and Yunnan in Western China.

With true Tibetan character, he hedged his bets by matching his military conquests with marital ones. He had both Chinese and Nepalese princesses as his wives, as well as two Tibetan girls from prominent families for good measure. With these alliances he secured his realm, but his marriage to the Tang dynasty princess, Wen Cheng, in 641, was to lay the foundation for Chinese claims upon Tibet in later years.

Although Buddhism had entered Tibet 200 years earlier it had only a tenuous hold on the country, but now the two princesses converted the king to their faith and were instrumental in its spread throughout the East. With Songtsen Gampo's reign began an era of political and military greatness, and subsequent *Tsanpo* (rulers of Tibet) were to dominate Central Asia for the next 300 years.

Tibetan forces, under the famous *Tsanpo*, Trisong Detsen, captured much of China, including the capital Changan in 763, and parts of northern India and Nepal, Ladakh, Sikkim, and Bhutan, all the way to the Bay of Bengal, were also absorbed by Tibet. These remarkable conquests, as well as a decree requiring the Chinese to pay Tibet an annual tribute of 50,000 bales of silk, were once recorded on two stone pillars in Lhasa but the inscriptions were defaced by the Chinese in later years.

As well as introducing tea from China, which Tibetans drink in copious quantities, Trisong Detsen summoned the Tantric master, Padmasambhava, from Uddiyana (present day Swat). This patron saint of Tibet, who is sometimes known as Lopon *Rinpoche*, suppressed demons, performed miracles, and ensured the dominance of Buddhism with the foundation of the Samye monastery and its first Tibetan school, the Nyingma or Red Hat sect.

Songtsen Gampo sent one of his ministers, Thonmi Sambhota, to Kashmir to commission a script for the Tibetan language. After four years of study in seclusion the king emerged to proclaim the virtues by which his people must live. He issued a list of 16 instructions covering good manners, kindness, respect and honesty etc. One that would not be thought politically correct today was: not to listen to the words of women.

In fact, the position of women in Tibet has always been a good one. Hereditary estates and titles invariably pass through the female line when male issue fails, and it was not uncommon in later times for Chieftainesses to rule principalities after the death of their warlord husbands. The *Tsanpo* introduced an organised system of government and 'a great code of supreme law'. Some of the punishments, however, were unusual: for cowardice the offender had a fox tail attached to his back to indicate banishment from society, but for failing to rescue someone from the attentions of an angry yak the penalty was death.

Contrary to the disparaging view that modern Chinese hold of Tibet's ancient culture and sophistication, a minister of the Tang dynasty Imperial Court described the Tibetans in 730 as "endowed with energy and perseverance, and were intelligent, sharp, and untiring in their love of study".

Tibet also toyed with socialism at this time. Mu-ni Tsempo, the successor to Trisong Detsen, deemed that all the wealth of the country be divided up among the people. But the equality did not last and, after a while, the experiment had to be repeated. After the third attempt the king's mother tired of this charity, and poisoned her son.

The last of the great monarchs of Tibet was the devout Ralpa-chan, who ruled at the end of the ninth century. He, too, conquered the territories of his neighbours and promoted the cause of Buddhism, extending the priesthood and allotting land for their support. However, he appears to have pushed religion too vigorously and, at the age of 48, was assassinated at the instigation of his brother Langdarma, who was the head of the anti-Buddhist party.

Having assumed the throne, Langdarma tried to destroy Buddhism in the name of Tibet's native religion, Bon. His own murder at the hands of a pious and cunning lama, who disguised himself as a dancer to commit the deed and then escaped on a horse dyed black, is a legend still celebrated today in a *cham*. Called 'The Black Hat Dance' it is performed during religious festivals. Thus ended the dynasty of the *Tsanpo*.

The empire contracted and what remained of Tibetan territory was devolved to the warlords of individual provinces who fought each other for overall control. In the dark period of Tibet's history that followed, the spread of Buddhism declined, after the suppression by Langdarma, but in the 11th century two new sects were to be formed.

The great translator Marpa, who travelled to India three times to study under Naropa, founded the Kargyu School, and Konchok Gyalpo founded the Sakya School in the tradition of the guru Drokmi. With this invigoration of religious enthusiasm, the priests of Buddhism in its lamaistic form began to extend their influence. Key amongst these was the scholar Ringchen Zangpo who established 108 *gompas* (monasteries) throughout western Tibet and Ladakh.

The cho-yon relationship with the Mongols

Before taking on the Jurchid Kingdom of northern China (the Chin), Genghis Khan secured his western flank by conquering the Tangut Empire of Hsi-Hsia in 1209, and Tibet's northern border became vulnerable to Mongolian expansion. The warlords joined together to offer the Mongols tribute, and thereby avoid confrontation but although Tibet retained its autonomy in return for levies, it had to place its warriors under the command of a Mongolian, Prince Auluchi.

Having formed an alliance with the people of Liao-tung in northern Cathay, Genghis Khan captured the Chin capital of Yen-king in 1214 sending its Emperor, Wai-wang, into flight. Next he embarked upon his great westward conquest, slaying Mohammedans, Persians, Turks and all before him, to secure his influence and law (the *Yassa*) right up to the borders of Europe. But he spared Tibet.

The great Kha Khan, 'Ruler of half the world', died in 1227 and, twelve years later, the emboldened Tibetan warlords ceased their annual payments to the 'Black Camp' at Qaraqorum. The new Mongolian ruler, Ogodai Khan, despatched Prince Godan to exact punishment.

He invaded Tibet and deposed the warlords but, after burning the Reting monastery north of Lhasa and slaughtering 500 monks, the prince relented and sought religious education as penance for his excessive behaviour. In 1240, he summoned to his court representatives of the Sakya school of Tibetan Buddhism and, having been converted to their faith, Prince Godan persuaded the Kha Khan to give the Sakya hierarch, Kunga Gyaltsen, temporal authority over all of Central Tibet.

Thus the Sakya Pandita, Kunga Gyaltsen, became the first religious leader to hold political power. The outcome of their treaties was an enduring and unique priest-patron relationship known as *cho-yon*, which literally means an object worthy of religious offering–dispenser of offerings.

When Kublai Khan, the grandson of Genghis, assumed the throne in 1259 he moved the capital from Kharakhorum to Dadu (an area of modern Beijing) and established a summer residence at Kaiping, later named Shangdu (Coleridge's Xanadu), and adopted Tibetan Buddhism as his empire's state religion. He continued the precedent of *cho-yon*, and allowed his spiritual advisor, the Sakya lama, Drogon Choegyal Phagpa, to rule Tibet.

This hierarch, who was Kunga Gyaltsen's nephew, had considerable influence over the Mongols, and he managed to secure from the Khan a promise to cease the annual ritual of drowning thousands of Chinese subjects in the sea to control their population.

The Mongol Yuan dynasty was formed in 1271. Within nine years Kublai Khan had deposed the Sung Emperors of southern Cathay so all of China came under his rule.

The ascendancy of the Gelugpa sect

After the death of Kublai Khan in 1294, the leadership of the Yuan dynasty became fragmented, and its authority diminished. In 1350 the Tibetan king, Changchub Gyaltsen, replaced the Sakya lamas and broke the alliance with the Mongolian Empire. Controlling the majority of Tibet, he established a new monarchy, which was to rule as the Sitya dynasty for the next 250 years.

In 1368, China also regained its independence and established the Ming dynasty. Changchub Gyaltsen continued to promote religion, but discarded many of the Chinese and Mongolian innovations introduced by the Sakya lamas. The Ming emperors maintained informal relations with the Sitya court but showed little political interest in Tibet. They did, however, hold a spiritual respect for the lamas, and designated the leaders of the Tibetan Buddhist sects *san da fawang* (great kings of *dharma*).

In the meantime, a religious scholar called Lobsang Drakpa became disillusioned with the lax living and corruption of the Kagyudpa and Sakya lamas, and founded the more devout Gelug School of Tibetan Buddhism; the Yellow Hat sect. This was based on the earlier Kadampa tradition established by Atisha in the 11th century. Gelug means 'the virtuous' and its followers, who are celibate and usually vegetarian, adhere to strict monastic discipline and scholarship.

The sect became the dominant religious authority in the 15th century, and great monastic universities were constructed at Ganden (1409), Drepung (1416) and Sera (1419). Lobsang Drakpa was born in 1357 at the Kumbum monastery in Tsongkha (Amdo), and this great reformer of Tibetan Buddhism became known forevermore as Je Tsongkhapa – 'the man from the Land of Onions'. He travelled widely throughout Tibet and Ladakh to popularise his new teaching.

In 1447, Tsongkhapa's nephew and foremost disciple, Gendun Drub, founded the Tashilhunpo monastery at Shigatse. The Sakya practice was to pass inheritance from uncle to nephew, but when Gendun Drub died in 1475 his spirit was held to have passed to the son of a Mongol prince, born two years later. This child became his successor, and the Gelugpas now adopted the concept of reincarnation, which had been the practice of the Kargyu sect since the death of its leader in 1283.

While Tibet remained under the rule of its own monarchs, Gyalwa Sonam Gyatso, who was the second reincarnation of Gendun Drub, travelled to the Mongolian capital of Tso-Kha at the behest of Altan Khan. The journey from the Drepung monastery, near Lhasa, took seven months, and the lama arrived in May 1578.

At a meeting with the Khan that took place in the Yanghua temple, Sonam Gyatso expounded the merits of Buddhism, and explained the advantages of his sect over that of the older church. Altan Khan had defeated his enemies, the Oirat Mongols, and established the respect of the Ming Chinese; now he learnt that he could also claim to be the reincarnation of the great Kublai Khan, and thus gain further political advantage.

In his delight at this discovery, the ageing prince vowed to restore *cho-yon*, and favour the Gelug sect of Tibetan Buddhism. Furthermore, he bestowed on Sonam Gyatso the title *Dalai Lama Vajadhara*, meaning 'Ocean of Wisdom' and 'Holder of the Thunderbolt'. Since his two previous incarnations were similarly honoured, Sonam Gyatso became the third in a line of Dalai Lamas that endures to this day.

Altan Khan, for his part, received the title 'King of the Turning Wheel and Wisdom', and in 1586 he built the Erdene Zuu Khiid monastery on the site of Genghis Khan's original capital at Qaraqorum.

War between the Black and Yellow Hats

At the beginning of the seventeenth century Tibet was in turmoil again. After the overthrow of the Sakya sect, a fierce conflict for influence developed between the remaining two prominent churches, the Gelugpa and Kagyudpa lamas. In 1605, Tsangba Khan, who ruled the province of Tsang from his *dzong* (fortress) at Shigatse, ousted the Sitya dynasty of monarchs, and installed the Tenth Karmapa Lama on the throne.

The Karmapa is the leader of a Kagyudpa sub-sect, and is known as the 'Black Hat' lama on account of a mystic treasure given to the fifth incarnation by Emperor Yung lo. The magic hat is now kept at Rumtek monastery in Sikkim where it is confined in a special box to prevent it flying away.

Tsangba then declared war on all the rival religious movements and, over the next few years, killed hundreds of Gelugpa monks and sacked the Drepung and Sera monasteries. It was during this period of strife that the Drukpa Kagyudpa hierarch, Shabdrung Ndawang Nangyel, was forced to flee to Bhutan where he established the unified Buddhist state that remains today.

When the Fourth Dalai Lama suddenly died in 1617, at the untimely age of 28, it was strongly suspected that he had been murdered by Tsangba who then tried to deprive the Gelug sect of future leadership by prohibiting the search for his reincarnation.

However, at the same time Tsangba fell ill, and Lobsang Choekyi Gyaltsen, one of the spiritual descendants of Tsongkhapa, persuaded him that he was being cursed by the deceased Dalai, and that his health would be restored if he would permit the succession.

Shortly afterwards, Ngawang Lobsang Gyatso, the son of a peasant from Chang-gye in the province of U, was recognised as the *tulku*. He was to become the greatest of Tibet's theocratic monarchs.

Tsangba was miraculously cured, and allowed Choekyi Gyaltsen to bring the young boy to the Drepung monastery where he presided over the *taphue* (ceremonial head shaving) and initiation of the novice.

Tsangba died in 1631, and his son inherited the throne as well as his father's dislike of the Gelugpa. But as luck would have it, Gushri Khan, another Mongolian noble, this time the leader of one of the Oiran tribes, travelled to Tibet, disguised as a pilgrim, to seek religious instruction from the Gelugpa's most famous teacher, Choekyi Gyaltsen. He presented 2,000 ounces of silver to the Drepung monastery, and pledged his devotion.

After the breakdown of the Mongol Yuan dynasty, competing princelings were supporting different religious sects, and Gushri's archrival, Chogthu Khan, the King of Qinghai, was a patron of the Karmapa Lama and all the Gelugpa's enemies.

The sovereignty of the Dalai Lama and foundation of the Panchen lineage

Gushri Khan was in search of a religious cause and, in 1640, he returned to Tibet with an army. He defeated the ruler of Tsang, deposed the Karmapa, and installed the 23-year-old Ngawang Lobsang Gyatso in his place. His reward was a great mansion in Lhasa called *Samtrup Po-trang* (the Palace of Fulfilled Purpose).

With Gushri Khan's powerful patronage, the Great Fifth Dalai Lama now established his authority over the warlords and all his sectarian rivals to become the supreme political and religious sovereign of a reunited country. The Karmapa's 'Great Camp' in Tsang was destroyed, and the Black Hat lama was banished to Tshurphu monastery where the lineage remained until the Cultural Revolution when the 16th holder moved to Rumtek.

However, three lamas of the original Nyingma sect, Lhatsun, Kathok and Ngadak Chempo, fled to Sikkim.

They established Buddhism there, and consecrated the first *chogyal* (king) of Sikkim, Phuntsog Namgyal, in 1642.

Henceforth the Gelug sect was to enjoy an enduring dominance and, free from persecution, the Dalai Lama turned his attention to the trappings of power. He formed a centralised government in Lhasa and, enriched with the confiscated treasures of Tsangba Khan, ordered a great temple to be built on the site of the 6th century fortress of Songtsen Gampo.

Construction of the Potala Palace began in 1645. It was to take over 50 years to complete. With walls 30 feet thick in places, strengthened by pouring in molten copper, a magnificent structure was built for eternity. Surviving wars, earthquakes and even the destructive fury of the Red Guards, this vast golden roofed temple

The vast golden roofed Potala still floats majestically above the Himalayan snows – the Eighth Wonder of the World

still floats majestically above the Himalayan snows – the Eighth Wonder of the World.

Inside, richly worked walls of stone, cedar and teak, joined by hand without the use of a single nail, create a thousand rooms on thirteen floors. Once these housed 10,000 altars and 200,000 statues of deities.

Lobsang Choekyi Gyaltsen had been the teacher and mentor of Ngawang until his full ordination in 1638. To show his gratitude, the Fifth Dalai Lama declared his *tsenshap* (tutor) to be the incarnation of O-pa-me, put him in charge of the Tashilhunpo monastery, and conferred on him the title of *Panchen,* meaning 'Great Scholar'.

Choekyi Gyaltsen's three previous incarnations were given the title retrospectively, and the lineage of Panchen Lamas at Shigatse was established.

More importantly, the precedent was now set for the two spiritual authorities to be inextricably linked, with each being responsible for the identification and education of the other. Henceforth Tibetans have referred to them as the 'Sun and Moon'.

To use a Christian analogy, the different schools of Tibetan Buddhism (Nyingma, Kagyud, Sakya and Gelug) can be compared with the Catholic, Protestant and Orthodox Churches, and, in Church of England terms, the Dalai and Panchen Lamas would correlate to the Archbishops of Canterbury and York.

Over the years Tashilhunpo grew to become a formidable focus of power in the region of Tsang. It housed 5,000 monks in the main monastery and a further 4,000 in subsidiary ones, supported by 16 manorial estates.

Lobsang Choekyi Gyaltsen himself recruited 150,000 disciples, and lived to the miraculous age of 92. When he died, his body was placed in a gold *stupa* inside a great hall with a golden roof. It was to lie undisturbed for over 300 years as an object of devotion for the faithful. But, during the Cultural Revolution, the *stupa* was broken open, and the Fourth Panchen Lama's bones were scattered to the monastery dogs.

Relationship with the Manchus

When the Manchus conquered China and established the Qing dynasty in 1644, the Fifth Dalai Lama sent envoys to Emperor Shunzhi to re-establish the *cho-yon* arrangement with his new Buddhist neighbour and, in 1653, paid a state visit to Peking where valuable gifts and titles were exchanged. The relationship, whereby the Emperor provided military protection for the Dalai Lama in return for spiritual patronage, worked well for a while, but became challenged during the reign of his next incarnation.

When Nagawang died in 1682, his chief minister, Sangye Gyatso, was administering Tibet's temporal affairs. Fearing that news of the Great Fifth's death might divert the devotion of the labourers, who were still working on the construction of the Potala Palace, he decided to conceal it. In secret he identified the reincarnation of the Dalai Lama in 1685, but kept the *tulku*, Tsangyang Gyatso, and his mother hidden under virtual house arrest for the next 12 years. The Manchu Emperor was belatedly informed of the Dalai Lama's death in 1697.

Unfortunately, perhaps as a result of his long confinement, Tsangyang had no desire to lead a pious life. He preferred the pleasures of riding, archery, women and *chang* (Tibetan beer) to the study of religious texts and, when he reached maturity, refused to take his monk's vows.

As a result, in 1705, the Mongol Lhabsang Khan invaded Tibet, executed the regent Sangye Gyatso, and took the unorthodox Sixth Dalai Lama away to exile in China. However, Tsanyang died in Eastern Tibet before reaching the border and many believe he was murdered.

Later, whilst the Tibetans rejoiced that the reincarnation of the Sixth Dalai Lama had been found in Li-tang, the Manchu Emperor, Kang-hsi, tried to install an impostor in the Potala. To secure the authority of his candidate he sent an army to Tibet in 1718, but was defeated by the Mongolians. The Tibetan choice, Kelsang Gyatso, was placed on the throne as the Seventh Dalai Lama.

Although the Emperor accepted the appointment, he subsequently recovered his loss of face when two years later he sent a larger force to Tibet that ejected the Mongol army and occupied Lhasa. Having reasserted Manchu influence, the Chinese military garrison was withdrawn from the city in 1723, and *cho-yon* was restored.

This incident set the precedent for Chinese attempts

to interfere with the selection of Tibet's lamas. In 1725 an obelisk was erected opposite the Potala to record the pacification of Tibet and the domination of its neighbour. The inscription carved on the monument placed the name of the Panchen Lama above that of the Dalai Lama. In 1731 Emperor Guang-xu gave the Fifth Panchen Lama the title *Erdini* (precious jewel). At this early stage the Chinese saw the Panchen Lama as a tool to counteract the power of his brother in Lhasa.

For much of the eighteenth century, the Dalai Lamas had little control over secular matters, and the political administration of the country was left to lay ministers. In 1750, agents of the Qing Court murdered the Tibetan Regent, and the Tibetan people in turn massacred the Chinese in Lhasa. So, once again, the Manchu Emperor dispatched an army to restore Chinese ascendancy.

First approaches by the British

Demand for wool, silk, tea and, especially, rhubarb, which was only available in the East and was highly sought after for its medicinal properties, caused both Britain and Russia, under Tsarina Catherine, to make overtures for trade with Tibet at this time.

The first attempt by the British to set up a trading relationship was instigated by Warren Hastings, the Governor of Bengal, who sent to Tibet first George Bogle in 1774, and then Captain Samuel Turner of the East India Company's army in 1782. Both of them reached Shigatse but the new Regent, who knew that negotiation with the troublesome British would annoy the Emperor of China, allowed them to proceed no further.

During his four-month stay in Shigatse, Bogle befriended the Sixth Panchen Lama, Palden Yeshe, and gained his trust but despite support from this quarter, no concessions were secured. On his return, Bogle wrote of the Panchen:

> ... *about 40 years of age, of low stature and though not corpulent, inclining to be fat...his hair, which is jet black, is cut very short; his beard and whiskers never above a month long; his eyes are small and black ... His disposition is open, candid and generous. He is extremely merry and entertaining in conversation and tells a pleasant story with a great deal of humour and action. Not a man could find it in his heart to speak ill of him.*

War with Nepal

In 1777, the Panchen Lama went to Lhasa to administer the young Eighth Dalai Lama's final vows, and teach him the scriptures. But the Manchu Emperor was keen to solicit support for his political projects and, on the occasion of his 70th birthday the following year, he invited the Panchen to visit Peking. Accompanied by nearly 2,000 attendants, Palden Yeshe travelled across the Tangla Mountains to the great monastery of Kumbum in Amdo, where he spent the winter.

In the spring of 1780, he continued through Ningxia, Gansu and Inner Mongolia until he arrived at the Imperial summer resort of Chengde. Here, as a measure of respect, the Emperor was waiting at the gate to greet him and, in contrast to the reception afforded to the upstart representatives of the British Crown, the Panchen Lama was not required to kowtow.

Palden Yeshe took up residence in the Yellow temple in Peking, which had been built for the visit of the Fifth Dalai Lama in 1653, but shortly after his arrival he contracted smallpox and died. The Emperor donated a solid gold *stupa* to house the embalmed body, and built a second Yellow temple in his memory, which still stands today.

As the remains of the Sixth Panchen Lama were being carried back to Tibet, a dispute over the ownership of his treasures arose between his two brothers. Chumba refused to share the treasures with his other brother, a Kagyudpa lama called Shamar *Rinpoche*. Enraged, Shamar went to Nepal where he drummed up support for his cause.

In 1792, the Gurkhas invaded and succeeded in capturing Shigatse, but the Qing Emperor sent reinforcements to the Tibetan army, and Shamar's force was expelled. To punish him for this act, the Emperor ordained that Shamar should have all his property confiscated, that his monks should be compelled to convert to the Yellow Hat sect, and that his lineage should be terminated.

Clearly, this last requirement was not fulfilled

because there is a reincarnation of Shamar *Rinpoche* today. The present holder is at the centre of a dispute over the recognition of the latest Karmapa Lama. This dissident regent has refused to accept the child chosen in 1992, whom the Dalai Lama endorsed, and is promoting a rival candidate. The quarrel has led to suspicions of murder and such violence at the Rumtek monastery in Sikkim that armed police now occupy it to maintain order.

However, a second legacy of the Panchen Lama's death was to disturb the Celestial Emperor. The fact that the Sixth Panchen Lama, Shamar *Rinpoche* and Chumba, who became Mongolia's *Hutuktu*, had all been discovered in the same family of aristocrats from Tsang led the Emperor to wonder whether the process of these selections had been entirely straight. Believing that the trances of the oracle might have been influenced by bribes, he resolved to prevent any such skulduggery in the future.

Manchu demands and the introduction of the 'Golden Urn'

After the Manchu and Tibetan army had repelled the Nepalese in 1792, Emperor Qianlong wished to formalise his influence in Tibetan affairs in order to control his embroilment in further conflicts. He sent an edict containing 29 articles to the Eighth Dalai Lama, and those points perceived to be beneficial were adopted.

One of the arrangements that the Tibetans agreed

to was the official appointment of Manchu *Ambans* to Lhasa, a practice that had begun in 1728. These were not viceroys or administrators but personal envoys of the Emperor, ostensibly with responsibility for Manchu interests and the protection of the Dalai Lama only. In reality, they were to wield considerable power.

However, Emperor Qianlong also wished to have greater control over religious practices. His proposal that selection of great incarnate lamas should be conducted by lottery and be approved by the Central Government provoked an enduring conflict of interest. He presented a Golden Urn, from which to draw lots, to the Jokhang temple in Lhasa where it remains to this day, but the Tibetan Government was insistent that this important task should continue according to religious tradition. The Urn played no part in the selection of the Ninth Dalai Lama in 1808, although it has been used to confirm three of the last six holders of the office.

Manchu influence and the importance of the *Amban* dwindled during the 19th century, and no military assistance was provided when Tibet fought wars against the Dogra invaders from Jammu in 1841, and Nepal in 1855. The Dalai Lamas also lacked influence, primarily because, between 1806 and 1875, none of the four holders of the post reached the age of 21.

Witchcraft practiced by the Regents, who enjoyed the trappings of office, was believed to be the cause of such short life expectancy. It was possible to invoke death by writing the name of your victim inside a boot then, after uttering suitable incantations, throwing it into a lake. An alternative was to put the name, together with various potions, in an animal's horn and get a dealer in Black Art to perform the appropriate spell. However, the Chinese, who wished to curb the influence of the Dalai Lamas, were the more likely perpetrators of these untimely deaths.

2

British influence

The Great Game

The 'Great Game' was the name given to the clandestine quest for information in the huge expanse of uncharted, mountainous territory caught between the empires of British India and Tsarist Russia. Lieutenant Arthur Conolly of the 6th Bengal Native Light Cavalry, who tried to reach Khiva in 1830 disguised as a Persian merchant, coined the phrase. This unlucky player was beheaded after torture at Bokhara 12 years later. Many like him were to conduct dangerous adventures worthy of a G. A. Henty novel.

Following the assassination of Tsar Alexander II in 1881, internal unrest had been deflected by stepping up Russia's opportunistic pursuit of political influence in Central Asia. This was seen as a threat to British prestige in India and the rivalry between the two powers and hence the intrigues of the 'Great Game' intensified.

British influence

At the end of the 19th century, the espionage effort was led by Sir Charles Macgregor, the Quartermaster-General of the Indian Army, who wrote a secret book, *The Defence of India* that prophesied the invasion of Afghanistan and spotted Russians under every bed. But to protect India's northern flank the focus of attention turned to Tibet.

Tibet protected its mystical secrets by eschewing contact with the outside world. Since 1750 only three Westerners had been allowed to visit Lhasa: Thomas Manning, an eccentric English scholar in 1811, and two French Lazarist priests called Huc and Gabet in 1846. Subsequent attempts to reach the capital by travellers from Britain, France and Sweden had all been in vain, but in the late 1870s the Russian explorer Przhevalsky compiled a scholarly account of the city.

Przhevalsky conducted epic journeys throughout Xinjiang, Tibet, China and Mongolia, where he gave his name to the breed of wild horses in the Gobi desert, but while the British honoured him with their highest accolade, the Royal Geographical Society Gold Medal, his exploits alarmed the administrators in India.

It rankled that a Russian had been allowed into Lhasa and, unable to engage with the insular Tibetans, the Raj now despatched spies to gather information for the Imperial Government.

They trained native *pundits* to pace out exact distances, and sent them into Tibet disguised as pilgrims. With a compass concealed in their prayer wheels, and special rosaries for recording their measurements, the 'surveyors' were able to compile secret maps of the country. The only reward for these hazardous assignments, undertaken in the service of the Queen Empress, was a gold watch from the Royal Geographical Society.

However, in 1885 there was a promising development that failed to materialise. Colman Macaulay, a secretary of the Government of Bengal, obtained Chinese consent to conduct a mission to Lhasa, but he had only consulted with junior Tibetan officials on the frontier and had failed to secure any authorisation from the Tibetan Government. There was a diplomatic row, and the plan was eventually abandoned in return for a concession in the newly annexed province of Upper Burma.

In 1887, the Tibetans sent a force to occupy Ling-tu, a mountain stronghold 18 miles inside the Sikkim border, in order to discourage any further uninvited visits to Tibet. They were directed to do this by the Nechung *kuden* (oracle), who declared that supernatural influences inside the fort would disarm any troops that tried to depose them. Sikkim had been an independent Buddhist kingdom with strong links to Tibet, but in 1861 the British had annexed some of its southern territory, including Darjeeling, and now considered the whole country to be under their protection.

Britain took no military action at first, but approached the Chinese Government to compel the Tibetans to leave. This line of communication failed and, following an ultimatum to the 13th Dalai Lama, Thubten Gyatso, troops were sent to the frontier to drive the Tibetans out. A British force, under the command of General Graham, attacked the *dzong*, defeated the Tibetans in three engagements, and advanced 12 miles across the frontier into the Chumbi Valley. The oracle was dismissed for false prophecy.

After the Sikkim incident the British Government in India, under pressure from powerful trading lobbies in both Whitehall and Calcutta, tried to set up a Trade Agent in Tibet. The negotiations faced every kind of evasion and made little progress. In 1890, a Treaty was signed that recognised a British Protectorate over Sikkim and delineated the border with Tibet at the Teesta River.

Three years later a Trade Treaty established an Agency ('mart') at Yatung in the Chumbi Valley, eight miles inside Tibet. But Britain and China were the only signatories to these agreements and the Tibetans, who had been excluded, understandably refused to recognize them. As far as they were concerned what the *Kaiser-i-Hind* (Queen Victoria) and the tottering Son of Heaven agreed between themselves was no basis for legislation of Tibetan affairs.

Attempts to develop the mart were frustrated by obstructiveness, and the boundary pillars on the Sikkim-Tibet frontier were destroyed as quickly as they could be erected. British India's dissatisfaction with its irksome northern neighbour intensified, and the race with Russia to secure a foothold in Tibet was on.

Invasion by the British

The Manchu dynasty had failed to protect Tibet from

external aggression since 1840, and the Dalai Lama's search for a more effective military sponsor was watched with interest by Britain. In particular, the activities of a monk called Agvan Dorjiev, who visited Moscow in 1898 and 1901 as the Dalai Lama's envoy, aroused British suspicions that Russia was winning the contest for influence. Already 150 Russian rifles had been sent to the arsenal in Lhasa, and there were rumours that a detachment of Cossacks was on its way.

Dorjiev, a former tutor of the Dalai Lama, was a Buriat Mongol who had made his way to Tibet and joined the Drepung monastery at the age of 19. But, since his homeland, on the shores of Lake Baikal, had been absorbed into the Russian Empire in the previous century, he was a subject of the Tsar. The Russo-phobic hawks in the Indian administration now demanded action.

The Viceroy of India, Lord George Curzon attempted to correspond with the Tibetan leader, but his letters, which had been sent via a Bhutanese emissary called Ugyen Kazi, were returned unopened. So, in 1903, he dispatched Captain Francis Younghusband C.I.E. on an expedition to establish a dialogue with the Tibetans, with the aim of compelling them to cease their dealings with Russia and to enter into a trading relationship with Britain.

Younghusband, who had made his name as one of Sir Charles Macgregor's intelligence gatherers, took as his interpreter Captain Frank O'Connor. This officer of an artillery regiment in Darjeeling was a close friend of

Rudyard Kipling, and had become captivated by Tibet, learnt its language and gained inside information during illicit shooting trips across the border. His knowledge was to prove invaluable.

After a period of preparation in Gantok, Younghusband, accompanied by Claude White who was the Political Officer of Sikkim and 500 sepoys from the 32nd Sikh Pioneers, crossed over the Kangra *la* and encamped at the foot of Khamba *Dzong* inside Tibet. On 18 July, he set up a conference with the envoys of the Dalai Lama: Lobsang Trinley, his *Trungche* (Chief Secretary); a senior *Depon* (General) Tsarong Wangchuk Gyalpo; and the Chinese representative at Shigatse, Ho Kuang Hsi.

Younghusband made clear British dissatisfaction at the Viceroy's returned letters and the border violations on the Sikkim frontier, but the Tibetans refused to discuss anything until his party left their territory. Then, to his great consternation, his interlocutors disappeared into the fort in a sulk and refused to come out.

There was a glimmer of hope on 21 August when the Abbot of Tashilhunpo and his retinue arrived. But this affable character was only interested in a metaphysical debate (he insisted the world was not only flat but triangular-shaped), and could offer no practical suggestions for breaking the impasse beyond a British withdrawal followed by the prospect of talks.

The Tibetan strategy was to procrastinate and wait for winter, refusing to accept any diplomatic communications and hoping the problem would disappear. With no delegates with whom to negotiate, Younghusband was out-manoeuvred and, after two months of frustration, was forced to abort his mission.

The Tibetans had tweaked the Lion's tail and the paranoid Curzon believed that only a secret treaty with the Tsar could have been the cause of such bravado. He embellished the Tibetan's villainy and the Russian threat to India, and finally persuaded the Balfour Government in London to sanction an advance into Tibet as far as Gyantse "for the sole purpose of obtaining satisfaction".

Younghusband, promoted to Colonel and appointed Commissioner for Tibetan Frontier Matters, retired to the Rockville Hotel in Darjeeling to prepare a full-scale invasion of Tibet. This time the Tibetans would face the might of the British Empire.

His escort (to be commanded by Brigadier General Macdonald) was augmented with British troops from the Royal Artillery, the 1st Battalion the Norfolk Regiment and 2nd Sappers, as well as eight companies of 23rd Sikhs and six companies of 8th Gurkhas. Six camels, 3,000 ponies, 5,000 yaks, 5,000 bullocks, 7,000 mules and 10,000 coolies were pressed into service to carry the baggage and equipment.

On 13 December 1903, Younghusband, with a single mounted orderly bearing a Union Jack, crossed into Tibet. Behind him a column of soldiers struggled over the 17,000 foot Jelap *la,* debilitated by *ladug* (altitude sickness) and temperatures 30° below freezing. The expedition advanced to Tuna, near Phari *Dzong,* where they waited for nearly three months in the desolate wasteland for supplies and reinforcements to be brought laboriously over the passes from Sikkim.

It had been hoped that the size of the British force would deter any opposition but the plucky defenders, who had again been told by their monks that magic would protect them, put up a fierce resistance whenever they were encountered. Younghusband immediately set about trying to secure a peaceful settlement, but all attempts at negotiation were fruitless.

Back in Lhasa, Shatra *Shappe*, one of the lay ministers of the *Kashag* (the Dalai Lama's Council) who had spent some time in Darjeeling during the Sikkim incident, knew the strength of British resolve and advised that resistance would be futile. He was supported by his three fellow *kalons* (ministers) but the *Tsongdu* (National Assembly) had them arrested for treachery, and imprisoned. One was to drown himself in a fit of depression and the remainder were subsequently exiled.

A new *Kashag* was now appointed, which included Tsarong, the general who had refused to negotiate with Younghusband at Khamba *Dzong*, and the Tibetan army was ordered to confront the invaders. A force of *dob dobs* (warrior monks), Tibetan irregulars armed with matchlock guns, swords and slingshots, and a local militia raised from the district of Phari reinforced the Tibetan troops that had gathered at the village of Guru. There, the informal army, under the command of *Depon* Lhading, built fortifications across the road from Tuna and dug in.

British influence

At the end of March, the British marched towards the Tibetan's camp at Guru. With overwhelmingly superior forces they took up attack positions at Chumi Shengo, and Younghusband, Macdonald and O'Connor rode out to persuade the *Depon* to surrender. But then a tragic incident turned the bloodless victory into a shockingly brutal slaughter.

As the Pioneers began to disarm his men, Lhading suddenly jumped on his pony and shouting hysterically charged the nearest sepoy shooting him in the face. The British, who by now had surrounded the Tibetans, opened fire with their Maxim guns. The unfamiliar warriors could not comprehend the effectiveness of high velocity bullets and, believing they would be saved by their faith, made no attempt to take cover or run away.

At the end of the encounter the British had suffered just six casualties, but 628 Tibetans lay dead. Those Tibetans who were wounded or taken prisoner were as equally mystified by the good treatment they received at the hands of the British in the aftermath of such ferocity.

With this unhappy encounter behind them, the expedition reached Gyantse on 12 April and camped a mile south of the deserted *dzong* at Changlo, an aristocrat's compound by the Nyang river. Here attempts to discuss terms for surrender were resumed. This time the Chinese *Amban*, an ineffective man named Yu-t'ai, was used as an intermediary but the British negotiators faced the inevitable Tibetan wall of silence as before.

Exasperated by the refusal of the *Kashag* to

negotiate, synonymous with the situation at Khamba *Dzong* the previous year, Younghusband was determined not to be thwarted this time. And, with the justification that the remit of his mission "to obtain satisfaction" had not been fulfilled; he demanded authority to proceed to Lhasa. A flurry of telegrams between Simla (the summer residence of the British Indian Government), London and Darjeeling were exchanged, and Younghusband was recalled to Yatung for talks with his masters.

In his absence the Tibetans reoccupied Gyantse *Dzong* and infiltrated the surrounding villages, and now Changlo came under siege. A British relief force arrived on 28 June and a fierce battle ensued. The Tibetans fought bravely but were no match for the modern weaponry of the British and the *dzong* was retaken with the help of a lucky artillery shot that blew up the magazine. O'Connor was wounded in the shoulder during the action.

It was clear that the massacre at Chumbi Shengo had done nothing to subdue the Tibetans' will, and that they would continue to resist the mission. So, reluctantly, the British Government granted Younghusband permission to proceed to Lhasa. He sent a final ultimatum to the *Kashag*, which was returned unopened, and the expedition marched towards the capital.

There was a last skirmish at Karo *la* - which at 18,500 feet must be the highest engagement in military history - and the British force reached Nagartse, on the shores of the beautiful turquoise lake called Yamdrok

Tso, on 19 July. At last the Tibetans began to realise the gravity of their predicament, and sent Lobsang Trinley, the Chief Secretary, to join the discussions, which now included Ugyen Wangchuk, the Tongsa Penlop of Bhutan as an additional mediator.

However, on 30 July, the British discovered that the Dalai Lama had fled. Thubten Gyatso and his entourage were galloping over the plains towards the Mongolian capital, Urga (now Ulan Bator), where Mongolia's political and religious ruler, the Eighth *Hutuktu*, Jebtsun Damba, held his court. The journey was to take four months. With characteristic Buddhist mystique, Jebtsun Damba, a Tibetan by birth, had predicted the Dalai Lama's visit the previous year, which was an unlikely event at the time.

There was now a vacuum in Lhasa and the British considered the Dalai Lama's behaviour, which effectively stalled all further diplomatic progress, as cowardly. But, like the colours of a British regiment, the Dalai Lama had to be saved from any threat to his symbolic status as the embodiment of Tibetan identity.

On the first day of August 1904 Younghusband became the second Englishman in history to enter 'the place of the Gods'. Britain had conquered Tibet with the loss of just 40 soldiers and 88 coolies (mainly from frostbite and exposure) and the Tibetans had to dismiss another oracle. As the force of 2,621 officers and men marched triumphantly through Lhasa's west gate towards the Potala, they found the streets deserted.

To the dismay of the hawkish Great Gamers, there

Colonel Younghusband's troops enter Lhasa

were no lurking Cossacks or stockpiles of foreign weapons - the Russian bogey had turned out to be a phantom. However, the British had been right about Dorjiev. He was travelling with the Dalai Lama and was despatched from Mongolia to seek the assistance of the Tsar. In the event, the Russians, who were troubled by internal strife following their defeat by Japan, were reluctant to offer more than sympathy.

The British troops camped near the Norbulingka (Summer Palace) without incident, although they misinterpreted as approval the shouts and clapping that greeted the military bands, which is the Tibetan method of summoning rain. Younghusband established his headquarters in the house of a noble family called Lhalu, and was now ordered to conclude a settlement as soon as possible.

The *Kashag* lost their shyness and brought gifts of food to the British compound and, in due course, the Tongsa Penlop of Bhutan managed to orchestrate a meeting with the *Ganden tripa* (Abbot of Ganden Monastery) who was acting as Regent in the Dalai Lama's absence. This genial monk called Lamoshar Lobsang Gyaltsen, whom Younghusband likened to the lama in Kipling's *Kim*, had little knowledge of, or interest in, the real world and, although friendly, the negotiations were inevitably evasive and long-winded.

Eventually, the Lhasa Convention, inscribed upon a nine-foot long parchment, was presented in a formal ceremony on 7 September. The occasion, however, fell short of the decorum expected by the Raj. As the British delegation, resplendent in their full dress uniforms, cocked hats and spurs, tried to negotiate the steep smooth steps and passages inside the Potala, they lost their footing and slid uncontrollably about the palace. This caused the lamas to dissolve into giggles but their mirth turned to fear when a magnesium flash was used to photograph the assembled delegations.

Order was eventually restored and the great document, which allowed the Government of India to open Trade Agencies at Gyantse, Yatung, and Gartok in far-off western Tibet, was signed. A separate agreement imposed an indemnity of 7,500 lakhs of rupees (£500,000) on the Tibetans, to punish them for fighting against the mission. The debt was to be paid over a 75-

year period, during which British forces were to be permitted to occupy and administer the Chumbi valley.

A strategically important wedge of Tibetan territory between Sikkim and Bhutan was, for all practical purposes, now part of India. The Treaty gave the British a foothold in Tibet of symbolic significance. It ended Lhasa's diplomatic isolation, and sent a signal to Russia that Tibet was within the British sphere of influence. Moreover, despite the humiliation and loss of life as a result of the invasion, the Tibetans soon warmed to the *Inji* (Englishmen) whose disciplined troops did not loot, and parted with their Indian rupees in Lhasa's Bharkhor market with good humour.

A street song at the time went like this:

> *At first they speak of "Foes of our True Faith";*
> *And next the cry is "Foreign Devildom";*
> *But when they see the foreign money bags,*
> *We hear of "Honourable Englishmen".*

The Tibetans compared the British Expedition to a frog, considered by them to be a fierce animal because of its habit of jumping but benign in comparison to the scorpion. They recalled an old proverb: when one has seen a scorpion (the Chinese), one looks on a frog as divine. Tibet's sullen hostility had turned to cordial friendship. Ten years later, on the outbreak of the Great War, far from rejoicing in the difficulties of her erstwhile opponent, the Dalai Lama offered a contingent of 1,000 troops to fight on the side of Britain and ordered prayers for the British success to be chanted in monasteries throughout Tibet.

Curzon and Younghusband had become the founding fathers of a Tibetan cadre who served the British Raj from a remote outpost in Gantok (Sikkim) for the next 40 years. These 'frontier' men pursued the Great Game to protect the Empire's northern flank, but their over-riding feature was always a deep affection for Tibet and its people. Colonel Younghusband was knighted, and served as the Resident in Kashmir until his retirement in 1909. He never returned to Tibet, but his influence lived on in his trusted lieutenant, Frank O'Connor, who became the first Agent at Gyantse.

British attempts to cultivate the Panchen Lama

While the Dalai Lama was in Mongolia, suffering a difficult exile as the guest of the hard-drinking and promiscuous *Hutuktu*, the Qing Government took advantage of his flight to announce that he had been deposed of his secular powers and appointed the Panchen Lama in his place. So, after assuming his post as Agent, O'Connor set off for Shigatse to pay his respects to the Ninth Panchen Lama, Thupten Choe-ki Nyima. When they met, the Panchen Lama told O'Connor that he was delighted to renew the friendship, which he had established – in his previous incarnations – with Bogle and Turner and the relationship got off to a promising start.

O'Connor worked assiduously to cultivate an alliance with the Panchen, who then seemed the only figure with sufficient authority to rule Tibet. In September 1905, he arranged for the hierarch to be invited to India, together with the Tongsa Penlop of Bhutan and the Chogyal of Sikkim, to meet the Prince and Princess of Wales. Every aspect of protocol and etiquette had to be negotiated and the preparations were lengthy.

There was also a difficulty over timing because the Tibetans were unsure of the date. They use a lunar calendar, which is complex. The years are named after twelve animals: Mouse, Bull, Tiger, Hare, Dragon, Snake, Horse, Sheep, Monkey, Bird, Dog and Pig, which are suffixed by five elements: Wood, Fire, Earth, Iron and Water, to create groups of 60 years. Furthermore, a month must be added every three years to adjust for the lunar cycle.

However, all was eventually resolved and the Panchen Lama, with O'Connor and 300 officials and retainers in attendance, set off for India in December. A special train was provided to take them to Rawalpindi where the Panchen Lama was introduced to the Royal couple and to Lord Kitchener, the Indian Army Commander-in-Chief. He also attended a review of Indian troops and, during the march past of 53,000 soldiers, the Panchen Lama was worldly enough to send two of his attendants to the rear of the parade ground to check that it was not the same troops marching round in a circle.

The party then visited several sacred Buddhist sites, and were received by the Viceroy of Calcutta. After a second meeting with the Prince of Wales, the Panchen Lama returned to Tibet in February 1906. By inviting him to India, the British aim had been to show off the power of their empire, and the plan succeeded. He was dazzled by the Raj, quite literally so in the case of electric lights, which the Tibetans had not seen before and went to great lengths to blow out. But, as well as offending the Dalai Lama, the expedition infuriated the Chinese who jealously guarded their patronage of the Panchen.

In late 1906, the Political Officer of Sikkim, Claude White, visited Shigatse and was told by the Panchen Lama of his wish to be independent of Lhasa and to deal with the British Government direct. The following year, O'Connor proposed a policy that, if accepted, would have changed the map of Central Asia. He suggested that the Panchen Lama be encouraged to declare independence, and create a separate state in southern Tibet, ruled from his headquarters in Tashilhunpo monastery.

With a British representative and military escort in Shigatse, British India would have a friendly buffer state on its northern border from which it could ensure that Russian influence was excluded.

It was a visionary idea that might have been accepted a few years earlier but, with significant changes in the cast of policy makers in the Empire at this time, O'Connor's new superiors were horrified by the plan, and rejected it outright. O'Connor was relieved as the Trade Agent in Gyantse by Lieutenant Eric Bailey, another veteran of the Younghusband mission, in August 1907.

Conflict between the Tibetan cadre and Whitehall

A new anti-imperialist Liberal Government, elected in Britain after the Boer War, swung public opinion against overseas adventures and, when it became apparent that the Russians had harboured no serious designs on Tibet, Younghusband's expedition became something of an embarrassment in London. Lord Curzon had left India in 1905, and his replacement, the Earl of Minto, was a much less dominant figure.

By contrast, a strong character in Lord Morely relieved the Secretary of State for India. He was totally opposed to what he called 'Curzonism', and gave his support to the 'China hands' in the Foreign Office who blocked the 'forward' policies of the Tibetan cadre. From now on Whitehall would not sanction any extension of British responsibility in Tibet, and proposed to settle Tibetan issues through negotiations with China and Russia.

In 1907, the Anglo-Russian Convention brought an end to the competition for influence in Central Asia, and freed each from the menace of the other. Both sides undertook to withdraw from Tibetan affairs and the treaty laid the foundation for a co-operation that endured until the Great War. The following year, the British acknowledged China's 'suzerainty' over Tibet by means of the Anglo-Chinese Agreement. This obscure legal term, borrowed from the Turkish Sultanate, implies that one state has some control over another that is internally autonomous. Britain now undertook to deal with Tibet only through China, and agreed not to send British officers to Lhasa.

Encouraged by Britain's diplomatic withdrawal, the Chinese set about reasserting their influence in Tibet. Trade between the two countries thrived, with Tibetan wool, yak tails, salt, musk and medicinal herbs being exchanged for silk and over 7,000 tons of Chinese tea per annum.

A new *Amban*, Chang Yin-tang, introduced various measures designed to modernise Tibet's institutions, and bring both their administration and cultural practices into line with Chinese custom. The garrison of Chinese troops was increased to 3,000, and Tibetan Ministers were relegated to the position of puppets. He even tried to assert Chinese suzerainty over Nepal and Bhutan, which indicated the danger that threatened India if China obtained a firm hold over Tibet.

In eastern Tibet, Chinese troops occupied the province of Kham, and the Central Government proclaimed its political authority by declaring the Khampas to be Chinese subjects who must pay taxes to Peking.

Meanwhile, the Trade Agencies, which had not been particularly successful in their primary purpose, due to a Tibetan dislike for Indian tea, now became increasingly politically isolated. By 1908, the British had surrendered nearly all the benefits Younghusband had achieved and allowed China to fill the vacuum. The final blow came when Whitehall ordered the 1904 indemnity to be reduced by two thirds. To demonstrate their authority, the Chinese promptly paid off the debt for the Tibetans and all British Indian troops had to withdraw from the Chumbi Valley.

The end of *cho-yon* and declaration of independence

In September 1908, the Dalai Lama made the journey from Urga to Peking for talks with the Manchu Emperor and Empress Dowager of China. He considered himself their equal in accordance with *cho-yon* but they conferred on him the deliberately humiliating title of 'Loyal and Submissive Vice-Regent', and ordered him to return to Tibet and obey the commands of the *Amban*. He left Peking with a profound dislike of the Chinese and arrived in Lhasa on Christmas Day 1909.

Early in 1910, 2,000 soldiers from General Chao Er-feng's forces in eastern Tibet were dispatched to Lhasa. To justify this action, the Chinese claimed a need to reinforce their garrisons in order to police the trade marts, which was permitted under the 1908 Agreement. The Tibetans, however, regarded them as an invading army, sent to enforce Chinese control of Tibet and remove the Dalai Lama from power.

During their advance, the Chinese troops had sacked the monastery and temple at Ba-tang, and used the scriptures to re-sole their boots. This act of desecration excited Tibetan horror and attempts by the Tibetan Government to prevent bloodshed now became fruitless. Fighting broke out as soon as the reinforcements reached the capital and, on the night of 12 February, the Dalai Lama and his ministers set off for the haven of British India, taking with them as much treasure from the Potala as they could carry.

Tibetan soldiers, under the command of the 24-year-old Dasang Tsarong and armed with only 34 rifles, held off a force of over 200 Chinese at the Tsang po ferry across the Brahmaputra river, 40 miles south of Lhasa. This gave the Dalai Lama and his entourage a head start.

Chased across the countryside by the Chinese, the party eventually reached Phari where William Rosemeyer, who was responsible for maintaining the British telegraph lines in Tibet, gave them shelter. The following morning they rode to Yatung, where they stayed three days at the residence of the British Agent, David Macdonald, finally escaping over the mountains and across the Natu *la* into the safety of Sikkim.

From Gantok the Dalai Lama travelled the short distance to India and took up residence in Darjeeling, where the Political Officer of Sikkim, Sir Charles Bell, looked after him.

Bell took this unexpected turn of events as an opportunity to rekindle the aspirations of the Tibetan cadre. He knew that Whitehall would never allow Tibet to be taken into the British Empire but saw a strong and unified nation under the Dalai Lama as the best means to ensure the security of India.

However, when the Dalai Lama expressed his wish to travel to London to appeal directly to King George V, the King wrote to him to explain that he "regretted he was unable to interfere between him and his suzerain." The Tibetans were astonished.

In the Dalai Lama's absence, the Chinese again deposed him from his rule over Tibet and stripped him of his titles. In terms that were even more insulting than before, they stated, "... in the view of the Emperor, he had forfeited the right to be regarded as a high reincarnate". The Panchen Lama had refused the Dalai Lama's plea to join him in exile and now the Chinese summoned him from Tashilhunpo to take the Dalai Lama's place.

He is believed to have been reluctant to assume power, although his administration had cultivated secret relations with the Chinese and had offered no assistance to their brothers in the capital. The 10,000 monks of the Drepung monastery also sided with the Chinese in a vain attempt to gain dominance, but their loyalty to Tibet improved after the execution of their leading lamas.

By meeting the Chinese in Lhasa and sitting on the throne of His Holiness in the Potala Palace, the Panchen Lama committed an act that branded him as a usurper. During the Butter-Sculpture Festival, where he accompanied the *Amban* in a procession around Lhasa carried in a palaquin, which was the exclusive right of the Dalai Lama, he earned only disgust from the public. Realising his folly, he soon returned to his monastery.

Throughout Tibet, the concept of Chinese guardianship, and hence its right to hold influence there, was evaporating. The failure of China to halt the advance of the British in 1904 revealed its impotence to protect Tibet against a foreign foe, and the sacrilegious behaviour of Chinese troops during their advance on Lhasa showed them to be the implements of an evil aggressor.

The *Ambans*, who had served to impress the unsophisticated Tibetans of earlier times, now aroused feelings of anger and ridicule and by threatening the Dalai Lama's life, the Manchus had violated the very foundation of their relationship. Having abandoned their attempt to put the Panchen Lama on the throne, the Chinese now offered the Dalai Lama the opportunity to resume his spiritual but not his temporal position.

The Dalai Lama, who distrusted them completely, refused to discuss it. He said that henceforth he would negotiate with the Chinese only through the good offices of the British. The era of *cho-yon* had finally come to an end.

By this time, however, the Qing dynasty was in trouble. Ever since the Opium Wars of 1842 and 1860, the Manchu Court had been too feeble to resist an endless series of treaties that ceded control of various regions and ports to European powers. These violations of Chinese sovereignty, together with a fervent distrust of Christian missionaries, inflamed xenophobic sentiment. At the turn of the century, support for the secret society of 'Boxers', a zealous religious sect that vowed to eradicate *yang kuei-tzu* (foreign devils), spread like wildfire throughout China.

In 1898, the Empress Dowager had deposed her

nephew, Emperor Kuang Hsu, and installed herself as Regent. While the weak Emperor remained the titular head of the dynasty, it was Empress Tzu-Tsi who controlled events. The bloody massacre of Westerners and Chinese Christians by the Boxers escalated to open warfare in 1900 and, while feigning concern in the presence of foreign ambassadors, the Empress welcomed the plight of those who had humiliated China.

She condoned the Boxer Rising in secret and ordered imperial troops to engage the multi-national force, commanded by a British Admiral, which had been sent to relieve the Legations under siege in Peking. Her patronage of the murderers was, in terms of diplomacy, as inexplicable as it was suicidal for the doomed dynasty and when the Allies entered the city her government was dissolved.

The Empress Dowager and her retinue fled to Sian, leaving a vacuum in the capital. Order was restored, albeit tenuously, but when the Court returned to Peking in late 1901, the large indemnity imposed on China after the rebellion and the punishment of those responsible caused further loss of face for the Manchus. Respect for the throne began to wane.

When the powerful Empress Tzu-Hsi died in 1908, her successor was a young child named Pu Yi, and, although the Manchu Court retained its spiritual importance, it lost all political influence. Confined to the Forbidden City and surrounded by an army of corrupt retainers and eunuchs, the Last Emperor's reign was to last just three years.

In November 1911, a revolution ended 3,000 years of Imperial rule in China. The Republican movement, led by Sun Yat-sen, forced the five-year-old 'Lord of Ten Thousand Years' to abdicate the Dragon Throne, removing the monarchy once and for all.

Command and organisation of the Chinese forces in Tibet now became fragmented and, as discipline broke down, they embarked on an orgy of looting. Chinese troops in Lhasa rose against their Imperial officers, killing their commander, Chao Erh-feng, and there was distrust and chaos on both sides as Monarchist and Republican Chinese, and pro- and anti-Chinese Tibetans, were pitted against each other in armed conflict.

The time was ripe to overcome the invaders. The Tibetan army approached Britain for military aid, which was denied but they received a shipment of rifles from Russia. Under the command of Dasang Tsarong, who had been made *Chida* (Commander General) by the Dalai Lama, they began to gain the upper hand. All supplies to the Chinese were cut, which led to starvation of the troops - some units were even found to have resorted to cannibalism. Thus the Chinese were broken.

In September 1912, the last stronghold in Lhasa was defeated and, three months later, the Dalai Lama returned to the capital. Nepalese mediation between Tibet and China resulted in the formal surrender and expulsion of all Chinese troops.

Basil Gould accompanied the Dalai Lama on his return journey from Sikkim to Lhasa and the party stayed a few nights with David Macdonald in Gyantse en route. Later, the Dalai Lama admitted that he had initially thought the British a heathen race but, having seen the number of Christian churches in India, he felt Tibetans had more in common with them than with the irreligious Chinese, who showed only contempt for the sacred objects of Tibet.

On 14 February 1913, the Dalai Lama issued a declaration reaffirming independence, and Mongolia and Nepal concluded formal treaties of recognition. The shaky Chinese Republic, which was headed by the unattractive figure of Yuan Shikai, who cast himself in the role of emperor, was in no position to counter the proclamation.

Mongolia later made a similar declaration and, with Russian support, succeeded in maintaining independence from China. Britain, however, noted with some unease that Agvan Dorjiev had signed a mutual-aid agreement with Mongolia on behalf of the Tibetans and they put pressure on the Dalai Lama to expel him from his court. Dorjiev left Mongolia for Russia soon after and he died in one of Stalin's gulags in 1938.

At the Simla Convention in 1914, the British attempted to achieve a settlement that would guarantee Tibetan autonomy. They surrendered their influence in Tibet in return for the region of Tawang, an outcrop of Tibetan territory bordering eastern Bhutan, which is now the Indian state of Arunachal Pradesh. This secured for the Raj a buffer zone of uninterrupted British influence the breadth of India's northern border.

British influence

The treaty recognised Chinese suzerainty and allowed the return of an *Amban* to Lhasa with an escort of 300 troops but only on condition that he did not interfere in the internal administration of Tibet. China was willing to acknowledge this but disagreed over frontier issues on the Kham border and refused to ratify the treaty.

Despite the inconclusive nature of the agreement and the Dalai Lama's dissatisfaction at having to cede Tawang, Lhasa was now able to function as an independent government. Britain acknowledged this with a new agreement on trade, revoking the two previous treaties made with China in 1893 and 1908. The existing Trade Agents at Gyantse and Yatung were retained. China, Nepal, Bhutan, India, Russia and Britain maintained diplomatic Missions in the capital.

However, although Britain allowed Tibetan administration to continue in Tawang, its loss was never accepted by Tibet or China and it became an important issue behind the Sino-Indian war in 1962.

For the time being, China was weak but although its various regimes disagreed over many things, about Tibet they were unanimous in their ambition to establish Chinese rule.

3

The Ninth Panchen Lama

The 13th Dalai Lama was a visionary leader who knew that the Tibetan way of life could not survive without reform. He also saw the need to improve the military in order to deter the Chinese from aggression.

Although Tibet under his rule attempted to shake off its medieval ways, with political reforms and a more democratic constitution, little real progress was made. The Tibetans had no enthusiasm for modernisation and the mood for change merely inflamed ambitions that led to bloodshed and cruel recriminations.

The system of tenancy and tax levies was corrupt, with each level of administration collecting more than the requisite amount and pocketing the difference. But even the peasants were content with this arrangement for they believed that by leading a pious existence and undertaking pilgrimages they would be reborn into a better realm or a higher *rik* (social position) in the next life. Conversely, bad behaviour might result in reincarnation

The 13th Dalai Lama was a visionary leader

as an animal, or worse still in the hell realm.

For uncharitable or greedy landlords, reincarnation as a *Yi-das* lay in store. These are fat, mythical beasts with mouths so small they are tormented by perpetual hunger and thirst. Once their evil karma has been expunged, they return to earth as locusts, a creature whose appetite is never satisfied. Hence there was little resentment of the nobility, some of whom were descended from siblings of former Dalai Lamas and measures to curb corruption were seen by Tibetans as unfairly denying them the opportunity for benefits in the future. There was even a full-scale revolt by the monasteries against the reforming policies of the Dalai Lama. This was quashed but served to illustrate the strength of sentiment in some quarters.

While it is true to say that Tibet was feudal at this time, the priesthood from the Dalai Lama downwards checked any excesses by the landlords. Nobles and peasants alike shared entertainment and education within their households and it was essentially a benevolent society.

The Simla Convention had removed some of the restraint on the Tibet cadre's activities and, when Lord Curzon was appointed Foreign Secretary in 1919, the British renewed their attempts to show their support for Tibet. A few years earlier, Sir Charles Bell had arranged for four boys called Kyipup, Mondo, Ghonkar and Ringang to be educated in England at Rugby School.

He had hoped that these sons of Tibetan nobles would help to introduce western technology to Tibet on their return but the experiment was not much of a success. Kyipup became Lhasa's city magistrate and Chief of Police but he lost his job when one of the great pole structures erected for the celebration of *Losar* (Tibetan New Year) collapsed.

Mondo became a mining engineer but was forbidden from prospecting by the abbots who claimed he was upsetting the spirits.

Ghonkar went to the Military Academy at Woolwich and was expected to remodel the Tibetan Army but he fell in love with an English girl and died of a broken heart when the Dalai Lama disallowed the marriage.

Ringang was the most effective. He took a course in electrical engineering and constructed a small hydroelectric power station in Lhasa, which produced enough power to drive the machines in the mint. As all the equipment had to be brought over the Himalayas by porters, this was a tremendous feat of ingenuity.

The Dalai Lama was an enthusiastic supporter of scientific progress and, on an amiable whim, had two motorcars brought to Lhasa piece by piece over the mountains. The cars, which had the number plates Tibet No. 1 and Tibet No. 2, terrified the monks as he drove round the grounds of the Summer Palace.

At this time the Chinese were making armed encroachments into Kham, and a war had developed on the eastern frontier. Thus, in 1920, Sir Charles Bell's life-long ambition to visit Lhasa was at last granted when the Dalai Lama invited him to the capital with a view to securing British aid.

The Ninth Panchen Lama

During the Dalai Lama's exile in India, Bell had become a close friend and was the first European ever to receive such an honour. His highly successful mission spent a year in Tibet, during which he offered the Tibetans arms, military training and technical assistance to help them protect and develop themselves.

Bell also acted as an agent for Sir Francis Younghusband, who was now President of the Royal Geographical Society, and gained permission for an assault on *Chomolungma* (Mount Everest) from the Tibetan side. The British Team were allowed to set up a base camp at the Rongbuk Monastery and mount a number of expeditions to try and conquer the summit, until the fateful attempt in 1924 when George Mallory and Andrew Irvine lost their lives.

The British installed a telegraph line from Lhasa to Gyantse and assisted with the construction of the hydroelectric station. Lieutenant Colonel R S Kennedy, D.S.O., M.C., of the Indian Medical Service, introduced the vaccine for smallpox into Tibet.

The Tibetan army was also provided with uniforms, as well as ten mountain guns, 20 Lewis guns and 10,000 rifles. However, the cheerful Tibetans hated the drab khaki garb and, envious of the First World War campaign ribbons worn by their British instructors, they covered their garments with pieces of coloured cloth to "brighten them up".

The Tibetan language has no military vocabulary so all words of command were given in English and a revised Morse code had to be invented to accommodate

Tibet's 36 letter alphabet. British influence was assured when the Tibetans became so impressed by the regimental bands that they adopted the tune to "God Save the King" as their own national anthem.

An English School was founded at Gyantse under the care of Frank Ludlow of the Indian education department who was keen to respect local traditions. He encouraged the children to wear their *chubas* (traditional Tibetan dress) and gave photographs of the Dalai Lama as prizes. However, he did introduce one aspect of western culture: football.

Discipline on the field was problematic and the goal posts were frequently stolen for firewood but his pupils learned to love the game. He gave them shirts in the Tibetan colours and 'international' matches were held between Britain and Tibet - although the boys' long boots with curled-up toes, which were not suited to kicking a ball, disadvantaged the home team.

The school was a great success but, sadly, education did not receive strong parental support and, under pressure from the lamas, the Tibetan Government closed it down in 1926. Another English school was started up in Lhasa during the Second World War but the monks disbanded it after only six months.

However, the craze for football spread to the capital where a number of teams were formed to play against the Nepalese Mission. There was strong monastic opposition to this *chipa* influence and, some years later, when a game was interrupted by a hailstorm (an inauspicious sign), the religious authorities had their way, and football was never played again in Tibet. In Lhasa, special magicians called *Ngak-pas* were appointed to prevent hail; it would appear they failed in their duties on this occasion.

The rift between the 'Sun and Moon'

A matter of grave concern at this time was the rift that had developed between the Dalai Lama and the Ninth Panchen Lama, Thupten Choe-ki Nyima. There was already underlying animosity between the two hierarchs as a result of the Panchen Lama's behaviour during the Dalai Lama's absence in 1910. The Tibetan Government believed the Panchen Lama to be pro-Chinese, not least because his administration had refused to help eject Manchu troops from Shigatse after the invasion. The catalyst for the escalation of this feud, which was perpetuated by the Dalai Lama's councillor, Lungshar, for his own political purposes, was a disagreement between the administrations of Lhasa and Tashilhunpo over the levy of taxes to fund the troops in Kham.

The dispute became increasingly acrimonious and, when some of his officials were imprisoned, the Panchen Lama's position became untenable. After approaching David Macdonald, the British Trade Agent, who declined to intervene, in 1923 the Panchen Lama fled to northern China, taking two million pounds-worth of treasure with him. Those found to have assisted in his escape were arrested and flogged.

Chiang Kai-shek's Kuomintang (Nationalist Party) allowed him to set up an office in the Nationalist capital,

Nanking, for they realised that patronage of the Panchen Lama now gave China a golden opportunity to encourage the rivalry between Shigatse and Lhasa and thus to destabilise Tibet.

However, after a while, Thupten Choe-ki Nyima sought to return home on his own terms and began a frenzied diplomatic exchange that was to last for 14 years. Having met Prince George (later the Duke of Kent) in Peking in 1926, he made repeated approaches to the Government of India and Sir Miles Lampson, His Majesty's Minister at the British Legation in Peking.

In May 1927, he sent his official, Tsa Surkhang, to India to remind Major Eric Bailey, the Political Officer of Sikkim, of a pledge of assistance offered by the Prince of Wales in 1905.

The British were keen for the Panchen Lama to return to Tibet in the interest of stability but, fearing the risk of incurring blame in the event of an unfortunate outcome, their answers to his overtures were friendly but non-committal. Bailey explained that, while he could not interfere in the internal affairs of Tibet, due to the long-standing friendship between the Panchen Lama and the British he would do what he could to help.

He wrote to the Dalai Lama to offer his services in bringing about reconciliation but received only a terse reply expounding the severity of the Panchen Lama's conduct and a reminder of the non-interference clause in the Simla Treaty. A plan to remove the potential danger of the Panchen Lama remaining in Chinese hands by offering him asylum in India was also considered but the

Government in India felt that such a step would rouse the Dalai Lama's resentment.

While these exchanges were taking place, the nephew of the Panchen Lama complicated matters by escaping, with some of his relatives, from his internment. The Tibetan authorities recaptured them in Shigatse and sent them back to Lhasa, where they were imprisoned, this time in shackles.

The next Anglo-Panchen contact was a letter written in 1930 to Colonel Leslie Weir, the new Political Officer of Sikkim, which implied that the Panchen Lama was recruiting a private army to return with him to Tashilhunpo. He asked the British to supply him with arms and ammunition, and indicated that he might use Chinese troops if the Tibetan Government refused to comply with his demands.

Weir, of course, would not help him, so the Panchen Lama approached some German firms in Shanghai that sold him over 1,000 rifles. He then raised a force of two hundred followers from the Sino-Tibetan borderlands and Mongolia and had them trained by the Chinese.

Although the British had always held cordial relations with the 'Tashi' Lamas, as they were known to the Raj, and had actively attempted to cultivate this one in 1905, they distrusted him now, and his insistence that an army accompany him on his return to Tibet heightened their fears of his intentions.

Meanwhile, the Chinese continued to make the most of the Panchen Lama for propaganda purposes. He was appointed 'Commissioner for the Pacification of the

Western Border', and statements were published in which the Panchen Lama was alleged to have expressed his hope that Tibet would resume its allegiance to the Central Government. Tibetans now believed that he had encouraged the war in Kham as well.

In 1932, Colonel Weir visited Lhasa for discussions with the *Tsongdu* on the fighting in Kham. The Tibetans wanted the British to mediate a settlement with the Chinese based on the Simla Convention but with a reduced military escort for the *Amban*. The Chinese refused to negotiate, but the situation for Tibet was eased by the outbreak of civil war in Sichuan. Finally, the efforts of the British Chargé d'Affaires in China bore fruit and an order was issued by the Chinese Government for the cessation of hostilities on their western border.

The Dalai Lama, who now felt that the Chinese might use the Panchen Lama's return as an excuse for further aggression, was anxious to put an end to their differences. In January 1933, he released all the Panchen Lama's relatives and officials from imprisonment and sent a letter to the Panchen Lama via the British Embassy in China. He wrote in friendly terms and invited him to send representatives to Lhasa.

The Panchen Lama's delegation arrived in June but the negotiations made little progress, on account of Choe-ki Nyima's demand for complete control of Tsang province, including all its troops and revenues. He even asked for the restoration of former Tashilhunpo estates lost during previous incarnations of the Panchen Lama from 1569 to 1882. The Dalai Lama was prepared to make some concessions but stipulated that the Panchen Lama must return by sea to India and thence to Tibet.

However, as the representatives prepared to return to China, the whole situation changed when, on 17 December 1933, the 13th Dalai Lama fell ill and died. Thubten Gyatso, the architect of independent Tibet, had "passed to the heavenly fields" in the tenth month of the Water-Bird year. The whole country went into mourning for the statutory period of 49 days. Prior to his death, the Dalai Lama had prophesied that soon all Tibetans would be enslaved and would have to endure endless days of suffering.

The Chinese Government appointed General Huan Mu-sung as 'Special Commissioner for Ceremonial Offerings to the late Dalai Lama' and the Tibetan Government agreed to accept his delegation to Lhasa. However, the real aim of Huan's mission was to secure China's designs on Tibet now that the Dalai Lama was out of the way. He asked the Tibetan Government to submit to Chinese authority and declare themselves one of the Five Races of China and a Republic, adding threats that the Panchen Lama supported this notion and would return to Tibet to enforce it.

After a meeting that lasted two days, the *Tsongdu* replied that Tibet had been ruled by 13 Dalai Lamas and would never depart from its heritage of a religious monarchy. They would acknowledge Chinese suzerainty on the return of Tibetan territory, namely Derge and Nyarong, lost to them on the eastern frontier but would never accept outside interference in their internal affairs under any circumstances.

Furthermore, they stressed that any subordination to China would only be considered within the terms of the Simla Treaty and the British would be consulted first in any discussion. This condition, which illustrates the esteem with which Britain was held at the time, enraged the Chinese delegation.

Huan returned to Nanking disappointed and recommended that the Government provide the Panchen Lama with an army as soon as possible to assist his reinstatement by force of arms. He left behind a small liaison mission with a radio transmitter, which freed the Chinese from reliance upon India's telegraph system and denied the British the ability to eavesdrop on their communications. However by so doing they attracted a countervailing British Mission, which was established in Lhasa three years later.

The struggle for Regency

A bloody struggle for power and the post of Regent followed the Dalai Lama's death. The key knaves in the plotting were Lungshar, the late Dalai Lama's counsellor, and Kunphela, his last confidante. Kunphela was arrested on a charge of being privy to the Dalai Lama's death and the *Chikyab Khenpo* (Lord Chamberlain), who had been responsible for the hierarch's safety, committed suicide by eating broken glass.

However, the charges against Kunphela were inconclusive and he was exiled, having narrowly escaped execution. The *Kashag* then summoned Lungshar to the Potala where he was seized and charged with attempting to subvert the Government and introduce a Bolshevist regime.

In his struggle to reach for a revolver from his servant, his arm was broken by one of the giant monk attendants of the *Kashag*. His official dress was torn from him as a sign of degradation and, when his boots were removed, two pieces of paper fell out. Lungshar managed to grab one piece of paper and swallow it, but the other was found to contain the name of the former minister and hero of Tsang po in 1910, Tsarong *Shappe*.

To harm one's enemy by treading on his name was considered black magic and it was suspected that the piece of paper now in Lungshar's stomach contained the name of the Prime Minister. His followers were arrested and confessions extorted.

It transpired that Lungshar intended to make himself King of Tibet, murder senior lay officials and cancel all the debts his cronies owed to the Government. He was found guilty of treason and blinded.

This traditional punishment was effected with a cruel contraption made from yak knucklebones, that squeezed the victim's temples until his eyes popped out; boiling oil was then poured into the empty sockets to cauterise the wound. In Lungshar's case the job was bungled and one of his eyes had to be cut out with a knife. Surprisingly, he survived the ordeal, and was kept in a dungeon until his release in 1938.

An unimpressive, cautious government that failed to

pursue the reforms begun by the 13th Dalai Lama emerged from this period of confusion. However, it tried to preserve the nation's independence by remaining on good terms with both Britain and China. The *Kashag* selected as Regent the 20-year-old *Rinpoche* who was in charge of the Reting monastery, the Fifth Reting Lama. He had shown exceptional ability as a child and was the reincarnation of a former Regent appointed in 1811.

Continuation of the Panchen saga

As soon as he was in post, the monks, who were keen to restore religious unity, put pressure on the Regent Reting to re-open negotiations with the Panchen Lama. At this point the Panchen Lama held the upper hand, he had received further titles and honours from the Nationalist Government, which he was quoted in the newspapers as praising profusely. The Chinese appointed Cheng Yun "Special Commissioner to escort His Holiness the Panchen Lama, the Western Borders Cultural Commissioner", assigning 500 troops to his base at Sining in Qinghai.

Full of confidence, the Panchen Lama sent a second delegation to Lhasa in 1935, with the arrogant message that refraining from increasing his demands following the death of the Dalai Lama was evidence of his eagerness to return. The Tibetan Government showed some flexibility by agreeing to restore to Tashilhunpo all ten *dzongs* confiscated after 1923. But it refused to turn over the additional districts of Shigatse, Namling, Penam, and Nangartse; permit the Panchen Lama to raise his own militia; allow Tashilhunpo to be governed autonomously; or permit an escort of Chinese troops to accompany the Panchen Lama on his return.

While Andrew Cadogan, a British Foreign Office official in Nanking, tried to put pressure on the Chinese to desist from providing military support, Frederick Williamson, who had replaced Colonel Weir as Political Officer of Sikkim, travelled to Lhasa to help break the deadlock. However, soon after his arrival in Tibet, he fell ill and died there from chronic uremia on 18 November 1935.

Sir Basil Gould succeeded him and offered to accompany the Panchen Lama if he would forego his requirement for a Chinese escort and accept the protection of soldiers from his own region of Tsang once he was on Tibetan soil. China, fearing that the negotiations might make progress, now declared that the sole purpose of the Panchen Lama's return was to cement relations between China and Tibet. The Panchen Lama refused the British offer and, with the build-up of troops at the Kumbum monastery, it appeared that an invasion by his force was imminent.

In 1936, the situation worsened when an alert border guard at Nagchuka discovered that a large advance shipment of the Panchen Lama's baggage contained rifles, hand grenades, and ammunition. Then, in March 1937, the *Nangmagang* (office of the Panchen Lama) sent an 'arrow letter' to Tashilhunpo monastery and to all District Officers on the way, including Lhasa's, instructing them to prepare all necessary arrangements to receive the Panchen Lama and his entourage, which would include 20 Chinese officials and 500 troops.

The *Kashag* were enraged by the tone of the letter and, above all, by the contemptible implication of the subordination of Lhasa. The argument had reached a crisis point. Negotiations over the escort, the authority of Tashilhunpo and the new Lhasa issue broke down.

Accordingly, in the summer of 1937, the *Tsongdu* ordered 1,500 troops from Kham to take up defensive positions in Rongsum southwest of Derge, and another 1,200 troops with five mountain guns to an area northwest of Dengo. In August, the Governor-General of Chamdo reported that the Panchen Lama had left Jyekundo for Lungshigon, a monastery within Tibetan territory. Then there was a remarkable turn of events that swung the balance in Lhasa's favour.

The Chinese had become embroiled in a war with Japan, which was absorbing all its energies. Too weak to risk what might become a costly war with Tibet, possibly supported by the British, they now became less sanguine over their promise of assistance to the Panchen Lama.

The *Kashag* seized the advantage and, believing they could now deal with the smaller escort that might accompany him, declared the earlier concessions to be their final offer. The Panchen replied that he had decided not to return to Tibet for the time being and would go back to Kantse in Chinese-held Kham. However, shortly after this, Thupten Choe-ki Nyima fell ill and when he died in December 1937, the exasperating affair came to an end.

The Chinese were robbed of a valuable instrument in their policy on Tibet and had missed a golden opportunity to establish a strong pro-Chinese Party there. They now switched their interest from the dead Panchen Lama to the more promising prospect of controlling the next Dalai Lama.

British military assistance

When Sir Basil Gould, who had escorted the Dalai Lama back from exile in India, travelled to Lhasa in 1937 to renew his cordial relations with the Tibetan Government, he took with him Brigadier Philip Neame V.C., of Indian Eastern Command, to advise them on military matters. Neame compiled a detailed report on the Tibetan army at this time, which was to have relevance later on.

There were nine regular regiments and 11 of militia, amounting to approximately 10,000 troops, in eastern Tibet. But many of these were on indefinite home leave. They had four mountain guns of doubtful condition, six good Lewis guns, and about 5,000 Lee-Enfield rifles. The militias were armed with swords and a motley collection of foreign guns and old Tibetan rifles.

In Lhasa there were 600 troops of the Bodyguard Regiment with six mountain guns, two Lewis guns, and modern rifles. There were also 4,000 new rifles and four machine guns in the government armoury at Trapchi. However, all the other districts, including those bordering Ladakh, were defended by militias with ancient matchlock guns.

All military training had lapsed after the death of the Dalai Lama and the most competent officers had been transferred to civil jobs. Furthermore, the procurement of ammunition from the arsenal was such an elaborate task that nobody bothered and the soldiers were unfamiliar with their weapons.

Neame's main criticism, however, was that the defence of the eastern frontier was flawed. All available troops were stretched along the border without any reserves to reinforce the threatened points and they were scattered amongst different commands, which received orders from Lhasa without local co-ordination. Neame concluded his report by saying:

> *"The Tibetan army is not sufficiently trained either in the use of their weapons or in tactics of attack and defence to enable them to resist a determined advance by even a moderately efficient army".*

He provided the Tibetans with a series of instructions for rectifying the situation which, had they been implemented, might have changed the course of history.

Gould urged the Government of India to provide military aid but since they were still awaiting payment for the last consignment of arms in 1920, his overtures were not met with much enthusiasm, although assistance with training and some wireless equipment was provided. Unfortunately the Tibetan Government then decided that the proposed restructuring of the military would provoke a confrontation with the monastic segment and it continued purposely to maintain an ineffective army.

The happiest outcome of Gould's visit for the Tibet cadre was the establishment, at last, of a permanent British Mission in the capital. Hugh Richardson led the Mission from a house called Dekyi Lingka, where a Union Jack flew above the building. He was instrumental in curtailing the influence of the Chinese presence in Lhasa until 1950 and continued to be a champion for the Tibetan cause until he died at the end of 2000.

The search for the 14th Dalai Lama

Besides the Panchen Lama dispute, the Regent's primary responsibility after taking office was to lead the search for the 13th Dalai Lama's reincarnation. While the embalmed body of Thubten Gyatso was sitting in state, the head was discovered to have turned from facing south to northeast. Furthermore, the Regent saw a peculiarly constructed house and the Tibetan letters *Ah*, *Ka* and *Ma* in a vision at the sacred lake, Lhamo Lhatso that lies at the foot of the mountains of Gyatsa. This and other clues supplied by the Oracle indicated that the region of Amdo (Chinese Qinghai) was where the boy would be found.

As religious tradition dictated, the Regent sent a large delegation under the lama, Kewtsang *Rinpoche*, and a high lay dignitary, Kunsangtse Dzasa, to seek guidance from Thupten Choe-ki Nyima, who was residing, in ill health and close to death, at the Jyekundo monastery in eastern Tibet. The Panchen Lama recalled an occasion at the Kumbum monastery when a small baby had refused to let go of the tassel he used for giving blessings and he gave the search party a precise description of the place where the 14th Dalai Lama had been born.

A child deemed to be the incarnation of the four-handed Chenrezig would carry signs that distinguished him from ordinary mortals, such as: marks of a tiger-skin on his legs; eyes and eyebrows that curve upwards; large ears; two pieces of flesh near the shoulder blades; or a shell-like imprint on the palms of his hands.

Guided by the Panchen Lama's directions, the search party, disguised as common travellers to conceal their true purpose, now went to the village of Takster where they found the house with a strange roof that the Reting Lama had seen reflected in the lake. It was the home of the two-year-old boy called Lhamo Dondrub whom the Panchen Lama had remembered.

The little boy was not fooled by the subterfuge, and demanded 'his' rosary and the other possessions of the 13th Dalai Lama that the lamas had brought with them. Astoundingly, he addressed the visitors in their Lhasa dialect, which his parents did not speak.

A few days later the delegation returned in an official capacity to examine Lhamo Dondrub again. He met some of the physical requirements and, after a series of further stringent tests, proved to be the current hierarch.

The Nationalists tried to hold onto the *tulku* and, before the boy could be released, a fee of 300,000 silver *dayan* (£23,000) had to be paid to Ma Bufeng, the warlord Governor of Amdo.

The 14th Dalai Lama aged four.

The ransom was advanced by a group of rich Sining traders and, once it had been paid, there was little Nanking could do except announce, rather condescendingly, that the child had been permitted to succeed by decree of a Chinese Government mandate.

In 1939, the young lama was brought to Lhasa, a journey that took three months. A magnificent celebration accompanied the arrival of the caravan and the Regent, who had the honour of shaving the boy's head (*taphue*), was given responsibility for presiding over the *tulku's* religious duties and education until he reached maturity. Three abbots: Simpon Khenpo, the Master of Robes; Sopon Khenpo, the Master of Religious Ceremony; and Chopon Khenpo, the Master of Tea, were entrusted with his care night and day.

In February the next year, during the celebration of *Losar*, Lhamo Dondrub was formally enthroned as the Dalai Lama and his new names announced: Ngawang, the Eloquent; Lobsang, the Wise; Tenzin, Defender of the Faith; and Gyatso, the Ocean. The Chinese had approached Britain to seek permission for Wu Chung Hsin, the President of the Committee for Mongolian and Tibetan Affairs, to travel to the ceremony via India, but it was denied.

The demise of the Regent, Reting *Rinpoche*

Reting *Rinpoche* then began to fall from grace. Greedy for power, he usurped the authority of his Prime Minister, Langdun, and applied to the *Kashag* for extravagant remuneration for his part in discovering Tenzin Gyatso. Corruption was rampant throughout the administration, with the Regent's friends ruling the roost, and the British, exasperated by his frivolous behaviour, withdrew their assistance to him.

While the Tibetans could accept his political manoeuvres, they were less tolerant towards Reting's nocturnal affairs. Faced with humiliation, he announced his resignation and retired to his monastery in 1940.

The *Kashag* appointed a new Regent, the aged Taktra *Rinpoche*, who had been a former teacher of both the Dalai and Reting Lamas. However, Reting continued to plot behind the scenes and even made approaches to the Chinese Kuomintang to help him regain control. His Sera monks rose in armed revolt and, after a failed attempt to kill his successor with a bomb, Reting was arrested and charged with mounting a coup. He was condemned to blinding, and his supporters were caught and flogged.

Reting's brother was given 250 lashes, but it was not uncommon for criminals to be beaten until they died. Reting, however, escaped the traditional punishment for treason; he had his genitals crushed and was poisoned by an unknown assailant. The Reting's great wealth was confiscated and his splendid house in Reting Ritro was razed to the ground. The inevitable Lhasa song went as follows:

> *Reting says he's a goat*
> *And is staying in a big corral*
> *Taktra's saying he's a tiger cub*
> *Has done in the goat*

The Taktra administration re-opened the issue of Tibet's military preparedness and, with the assistance of Sir Basil Gould, succeeded in securing some aid from British India. In 1943, a team of two officers and 16 soldiers were sent to Gyantse to train the Tibetans and a British ordnance expert went to Lhasa to re-commission the mountain guns.

Mules transported a large consignment of five million rounds of rifle ammunition and 1,000 shells for the guns over the mountains from Sikkim. But what Tibet really needed was more modern weapons, which the British declined to provide, claiming short supply due to their own war in the Far East. The truth, however, was that the Raj was reluctant to arm its northern neighbour too effectively. As a result, Tibet was woefully ill equipped for what was to follow.

During the Second World War, Tibet was little affected. Britain had secured a monopoly on wool from Australia, and the all-important Tibetan wool trade thrived with demands from America.

The Tibetan Government confined itself to neutral aspirations for the restoration of peace but, in 1942, sent a message of congratulation to Britain following victory in North Africa. There was also a general feeling of sympathy for Chinese suffering during the Sino-Japanese war, although the Allies were not allowed to send supplies from India to China via Tibet. At the end of the war, Tibet sent a delegation to the Viceroy of India, Lord Wavell, with gifts and praises for the Allied victory.

4

The Tenth Panchen

Identification, enthronement and abduction by the Chinese

It should come as no surprise that the search for the reincarnation of the Ninth Panchen Lama was problematic. The Council of Khenpo, the highest authority of Tashilhunpo, supervised the process, which is shrouded in arcane religious lore.

It began in the summer of 1938, when a delegation, led by Bilung *Rinpoche*, went to the sacred lake Lhamo Lhatso for inspiration. Here the traditional offerings and rituals, which involve burning cypress and sandalwood branches on the shore of the lake and chanting *mantras,* were rewarded by an abundance of extraordinary climatic phenomena and apparitions.

The *Rinpoche* and G*eshe* (doctor of Buddhist philosophy) recorded the visions they had seen independently and sealed their findings for the Dalai Lama to interpret. However, since Tenzin Gyatso was only three, the parchments were handed to the Regent Reting, and several years were to elapse before the contents were read.

The Chinese Nationalists now saw the advantage of their involvement in the selection process, and tried to influence the outcome by clandestine means. They also prepared the ground to set up the new Panchen Lama as a temporal power in Tibet should they be successful in securing a puppet. The Chinese Year Book of 1943 contains propaganda suggesting that the Panchen Lama has the right to be considered as a possible ruler of Tibet.

The direction of the priests' prostrations at the lake, and the trances of the Nechung *kuden*, Lobsang Namgyl, indicated that the boy was to be found to the east, in the province of Amdo, just as the Dalai Lama's *tulku* had been. Delegations were despatched to conduct the search, and by late 1944 ten potential candidates had been found and brought to the Kumbum monastery.

Here the children were set a number of tests, which included the ability to recognise possessions of the former incarnate. However the first three to show promise died in mysterious circumstances, possibly at the hands of the Chinese, soon after impressing their selectors. Finally, Lobsang Gonpo Tseten, a young peasant who had been born in the village of Karang Bidho in Amdo on 3 February 1938, not only passed all the tests, but also was able to recognise members of the former Panchen Lama's circle. This may have been the result of Chinese tutoring, but reports by local people of visions at the time of his birth convinced the Council of Khenpo that he was the true reincarnation.

It was still necessary for the selection to be sanctioned by Lhasa, and the *Kashag*, which favoured their own candidate, had reservations over the short time between the lama's death and this boy's birth, a matter of only two months. There were in fact two other contenders, both born in Kham, who were residing in the Tashilhunpo and Drepung monasteries. Determined to resolve the issue, the *Kashag* summoned all three candidates to Lhasa.

Earlier the Kuomintang had advocated that the choice of Panchen Lama must be made official by drawing lots from the Golden Urn in compliance with the 'Twenty Nine Point' imperial edict of Emperor Qianlong, but now the exiled Panchen's circle was reluctant to release their nominee. Even if Gonpo Tseten was successful in the lottery, there would be no reason for him to return to Amdo and they would lose this bargaining chip for the restoration of the Tashilhunpo estates.

Gonpo Tseten and his parents were moved into the Kumbum monastery under the care of the Abbot who, coincidently, was the Dalai Lama's elder brother, and awaited the settlement of his destiny. Then in June 1949, Li Zongren, the acting president of Nationalist China, now on the brink of defeat, issued a mandate exempting Tseten from the Golden Urn ceremony and recognizing his claim. His proclamation declared that "by special authorisation" Lobsang Gonpo Tseten was to be the Tenth Panchen Lama.

The Chairman for Mongolian and Tibetan Affairs, Guan Jiyu, was sent to the Kumbum monastery to preside over the enthronement ceremony, which duly took place on 10 August, and the boy was given his religious name Choekyi Gyaltsen. The Chinese also appointed him Chairman of a provisional Government of Tibet in readiness to take over the throne if they gained control of the country and the Dalai Lama fled.

The *Kashag,* furious at having their authority usurped, refused to recognise Choekyi Gyaltsen. They closed the Chinese mission in Lhasa and expelled 350 residents. A month later the Nationalists were in flight.

Chinese Invasion

Bolstered by military aid from Stalin, Mao Tse-tung's forces defeated the Nationalists during the civil war and by the end of 1949 had achieved victory throughout most of China.

Amdo was the Chinese province of Qinghai but a regional government based in Sining ruled it autonomously. Ma Bufeng, the Governor at this time, was a Tungan of Mongol descent and also a Muslim who was loyal to the Nationalists.

In the summer of 1949, he had led the resistance to the Communist advance with the troops of his Muslim cavalry but they were finally defeated in the battle of Lanchou. After Chiang Kai-shek had fled to Taiwan, Ma Bufeng made good his escape too and, in September, he left Amdo for the last time, packing his wives and treasure on two DC10s.

A few days later the PLA entered Sining unopposed. Ma Bufeng had offered to fly the Panchen Lama to safety, but the Panchen's entourage preferred to take their chances with the Communists rather than face an uncertain future in exile. On 1 October, the head of the *Nangmagang*, Chen Jigme, sent a telegram to Mao on the behalf of his charge offering congratulations and the Panchen Lama's unqualified support for the Chinese cause in Tibet.

For his pains, the PLA seized the eleven-year-old boy from Kumbum monastery and sent him to Beijing, thereby providing the People's Republic of China (PRC) with a political pawn to exert pressure upon the Dalai Lama. The new Communist Governor of Amdo, Tang Tushi, gave assurances that the Red Army had come in peace and heralded the start of "better times" for Tibetans. But soon the true nature of *Chingtro* (the great Liberation) was to become apparent.

The monasteries of Shartsong Ritro, Serto Ritro and Tongkhor were ravaged by a communist-led mob and burnt to the ground. The local bandits called Hu-hus then attacked the Chinese at Lussar, and any idea of a benign occupation was lost.

On New Year's Day 1950, Radio Peking began broadcasting propaganda in Tibetan. In its first transmission the announcer declared that the task of the PLA was "to liberate Formosa (Taiwan), Hainan and Tibet from American and British imperialism". On 16 April, Chinese Communists invaded Hainan and defeated the Nationalists within a fortnight. Tibet was next.

Tibet's eastern border had been fought over repeatedly and, in 1918, the Tibetans drove the Chinese out of Mang-kam, Tra-ya, and Chamdo. This action was a demonstration of Tibetan independence at that time and a truce, brokered by Mr Eric Teichman of the British Consular Service in China, set the demarcation line at the Upper Yangtse River. Thus the region of Kham became the front line for Tibetan resistance to the invasion.

The nominal strength of the whole Tibetan Army at this time was 8,500 men, of which only 1,000 guarded the eastern frontier with a few Lewis guns and three pieces of ancient mountain artillery. Lhalu *Shappe*, who was the son of the blinded Lungshar, was Governor General of Kham and Commander-in-Chief of all forces in Eastern Command. He had an additional 500 men in the Chamdo garrison and a further 250 in his personal bodyguard, but such a force was pitifully inadequate to counter a professional army.

Lhalu was a realist who took practical steps to improve his defences. He succeeded in recruiting local volunteers from the Khampas; these proud yet wild, lawless people were fearsome warriors who were loyal to the Dalai Lama but ambivalent towards the Lhasa officials to whom they had to pay their taxes. The Khampas across the Yangtse in Sikang and eastern Qinghai had already joined the Communists and the allegiance of those on the west bank required careful cultivation.

The key obstacle to Lhalu's preparations, however, was the reluctance of the Government to face up to the reality of the threat and assure the world that Tibet would resist an invasion. Lhasa buried its head in the sand, and hoped that the gods would solve the problem. In Tibet each secular position of state (including high appointments in the military) was mirrored by an ecclesiastical one, and this was the senior of the two. The lamas believed that all that was required to defeat the godless Chinese was prayer.

Some were pragmatic enough to realise that the use of modern equipment would improve their chances, but an example of the difficulties arose in a discussion on the use of aircraft: the monks were adamant they could not allow the use of such machines in Tibetan airspace as they would disturb the spirits that dwelt in the upper air.

In June 1950, the Red Chinese entered Tibet and took the town of Dengko. They were subsequently repulsed but, despite this incursion, Lhasa still remained silent. In August, there was a terrible earthquake on the border with Assam, an inauspicious sign, and, later that month, Ngawang Jigme Ngabo relieved Lhalu. This new Governor was both indecisive and defeatist, and made no attempt to consolidate the preparations made by his predecessor.

On 7 October, Radio Peking announced: "People's Army units have been ordered to advance into Tibet to free three million Tibetans from imperialist oppression and to consolidate national defences on the western borders of China".

Around 40,000 well-seasoned soldiers of the 18th Route Army, led by General Zhang Guohua, crossed the

Chinese cavalry enter Tibet

Tibetan frontier in six places simultaneously, but the main attack across the Yangtse was at Gangto Druga in the region of Chamdo.

Robert Ford, the British radio operator stationed there, remained at his post to contact Lhasa with news and then smashed his radio to prevent it from getting into Chinese hands. But, despite this selfless act, which denied Ford the chance of escape, the outside world was unaware of the event. Indeed, eight days later, in a news bulletin from Delhi it was reported that the Tibetan delegation in Delhi had denied rumours of a Chinese invasion.

The poorly armed Tibetan defenders put up fierce resistance under General Muja but other Tibetan leaders were quick to capitulate. Ngabo *Shappe* and his Lhasa officials fled from Chamdo in the dead of night using all available transport. The Khampas and the remnants of the army were left to their fate without the means to conduct an orderly withdrawal.

A few days later in Lho *Dzong*, Ngabo surrendered all the forces in Kham to General Wang, the Commander of the Second Field Army. Eastern Tibet was soon overrun but, despite their betrayal, the Khampas fought on until 1952 when the Dalai Lama implored them to lay down their arms.

On 7 November, the Tibetan Government at last appealed to the United Nations, describing the Chinese attack as clear aggression. Britain and India were best placed to offer their support but shamefully abrogated this responsibility by advising the United Nations General Assembly not to take action for the time being.

Ernest Bevin, the Labour Foreign Secretary, stated that the invasion of Tibet was not a threat to world peace and the British Government gave its support to Pandit Nehru, who naively believed that friendship with China was sufficient guarantee of India's security. An appeal by the Dalai Lama to the United States was similarly denied, and Tibet stood alone.

The Dalai Lama's eldest brother, Thupten Jigme Norbu, had been recognised in infancy as the reincarnation of the Tagtser Lama, and he was the Abbot of Kumbum at the time of the Chinese occupation. The two brothers had seen little of each other, and now Thupten Norbu arrived in Lhasa as an envoy of the Communists. His purpose was to persuade the Dalai Lama to welcome the advance of the Chinese 'liberators' without further resistance, and to accept the People's Republic as an ally. If successful, his former crimes would be forgiven and he would be made Governor General of Tibet but if the Dalai Lama did not surrender, it was suggested that he should kill him.

Aghast at the mentality of the Chinese to believe they could demand such a deed from a brother, Thupten Norbu nevertheless pretended to go along with the plan. Once inside Tibet, he broke free from his Chinese stooges and made his way alone to the Potala Palace. He was in a terrible state of nerves when he met with the Dalai Lama and told his brother everything, resolving to renounce his vows and flee to America where he would seek help.

Thupten Norbu's description of the treatment of monks in Amdo did not bode well for the future of Tibet or the safety of the Dalai Lama. Accordingly the *Kashag* decided to hasten the enthronement of Tenzin Gyatso as the temporal leader of Tibet, despite him still being a minor, and prepare for his escape.

On 17 November 1950, the *Tsongdu* invested the young Dalai Lama with full ruling powers and, as soon as the ceremony had been completed, they sent him to the monastery of Dungkhar that overlooks the Dromo valley on the Sikkim border. From this haven of relative security, the Dalai Lama's ministers monitored the steady advance of the Chinese towards the capital, and sent Ngawang Jigme Ngabo to Beijing to sue for peace.

On 23 May 1951, the Tibetan delegation in Beijing signed Mao's 'Seventeen Point Agreement for the Peaceful Liberation of Tibet'. As a further humiliation, the PRC used their new puppet lama, Choekyi Gyaltsen, to enhance their propaganda. After careful tutoring, the 12-year-old boy was forced to recite a speech praising Chinese occupation.

The agreement shocked the *Kashag* because Ngabo had been sent only to negotiate and, with the seals of state held by the Dalai Lama, he had no authority to sanction what amounted to a surrender of sovereignty.

In July, the Chinese sent a delegation led by General Chiang Chin-wu to Dromo to explain the 'Seventeen Point Agreement', to give the PRC's commitment of friendship towards the Dalai Lama and a promise to respect religious freedom. With these assurances, the Dalai Lama decided to return to Lhasa.

On 26 October, the first contingent of the occupying power comprising 3,000 troops of the Chinese 18th Route Army entered the capital and Tibet was in China's hands. The imperialists from whom Tibet had been saved amounted to just seven people: Hugh Richardson, head of the Indian Mission in Lhasa; Reginald Fox and Robert Ford, radio operators employed by the Tibetan Government in Lhasa and Chamdo; Geoffrey Bull, a missionary in Sikang; the Austrians Heinrich Harrer and Peter Aufschnaiter; and a White Russian called Nedbailoff. Ford and Bull were captured and spent the next five years in a Chinese jail, the rest escaped.

General Chiang Chin-wu became Governor General of Tibet, and there was a period of self-government, albeit under Chinese control, during which the country was essentially autonomous. Officials were allowed to keep their posts and the monasteries continued to function unmolested. But as the PLA garrison in the capital grew, Chinese oversight became oppressive, and the requirement to feed and house over 20,000 troops became more debilitating for the people of Lhasa. Bit by bit the promises made by the Chinese evaporated and tensions grew as the resentment increased.

The Tibetan Government was ordered to recognise Choekyi Gyaltsen's selection and, given the desperate circumstances, the Dalai Lama and his advisers relented. They quickly conducted a divination that conveniently reported that the candidate in Beijing was the true reincarnation of the late Panchen Lama. Of the other two contenders for the post, the Drepung candidate was accorded the title Panchen Outrul *Rinpoche* and fled to Ireland where he now runs a small religious centre, but the Tashilhunpo candidate was captured trying to escape and was never seen again.

The PRC now saw the triumphal return of the Panchen Lama to Tibet as a matter of urgency. In December 1951, Choekyi Gyaltsen, accompanied by his council of abbots, members of his family and attendants, began the 2,000 mile trek from Sining to Tashilhunpo.

This was a hazardous journey to undertake in winter and many of the 7,000 yaks, 3,000 camels, and 200 mules that carried the food, baggage, and treasures were to die en route. In April 1952 the caravan arrived in the capital where they stayed for two months before continuing to Shigatse. On 23 June, after an absence of 29 years, the Panchen Lama returned to Tashilhunpo at last. It was mid-summer, but snowflakes fell – a most auspicious sign.

Whilst the Panchen Lama was in Lhasa the Dalai Lama met him for the first time, and it is believed that

The Dalai Lama & Panchen Lama with Chairman Mao, Beijing 1954

the two teenagers formed a lasting, if wary, friendship. In 1954, they attended the National People's Congress in China and were appointed to high political positions. But the key purpose of this was to set in train the mechanisms by which Tibet would be assimilated into the political structure of the People's Republic. The Preparatory Committee for the Tibet Autonomous Region (PCART), which was formed under the supervision of Marshal Chen Yi, paved the way for Chinese administration, and essentially removed all power from the Dalai Lama's Government.

Two years later the two lamas, somewhat surprisingly, were allowed to travel to India for the 2,500th anniversary of the birth of Buddha on the tenth day of the sixth month. Whilst there, the Dalai Lama was temporarily reunited with his brother, Thupten Norbu, who had succeeded in getting to the United States at the invitation of the American Committee for Free Asia, and was studying English at Berkeley University. As well as running a successful campaign in the Unites States to publicise the plight of Tibetans and raise money for refugees, he had also managed to make contact with the Intelligence Services to solicit undercover military support.

Now he was trying to obtain the help of the Indian Government but this was more problematic. In 1954, Nehru had signed a Sino-Indian treaty that included a memorandum known as 'Pauch Sheel' which acknowledged China's right to Tibet, and secured an agreement that neither country would interfere in the internal affairs of the other. However, China's Foreign Minister, Chou En-lai, was also visiting India at this time, and Nehru did agree to support the Dalai Lama's appeal over the 'reforms' being undertaken in eastern Tibet. Chou pledged that any abuses that existed would be corrected, and the sycophantic Panchen assured him of his support for Chinese policy.

Tibet enslaved

Meanwhile, Chinese political manipulation throughout Tibet worsened; an attempt to incite the peasants against their masters was met with fierce resistance by the Khampas, many of whom were feudal landlords. In the spring and summer of 1956 a revolt broke out in eastern Tibet, and the activities of the Khampa-Amdowa freedom fighters, who cut Chinese military roads, blew up bridges and besieged the garrisons, gave Mao an excuse to hasten the total annexation of the country.

Large numbers of PLA reinforcements were sent into the region with orders to conduct a ruthless campaign against Tibetan defiance. Villages believed to be housing rebels were razed to the ground with artillery and an air strike was mounted against the monastery at Lithang. Women and children whose fathers and husbands were suspected of joining the resistance movement were subjected to merciless torture and then beheaded. But, in spite of such cruelty, opposition to the Chinese occupation increased.

A 24-year-old Khampa noble called Andrugtshang formed the *Chu-shi Gang-druk* (Four Rivers, Six

Khampa-Amdowa freedom fighters cut Chinese military roads, blew up bridges and besieged the garrisons

Ranges) militia, and co-ordinated a widespread guerrilla movement that was supported by the CIA with airdrops of weapons and equipment. Thupten Norbu had arranged American assistance, but to disguise the origin of the supplies, only old British Lee-Enfield rifles were provided, which were of limited use against the PLA's firepower. As a result, operations over the next 18 months were beset with heavy casualties.

In 1958 Mao launched the 'Great Leap Forward', a crash programme of communisation and forced industrialisation that was to wreck Chinese agriculture, leading to death by starvation of more than 30 million people. 'Counter-revolutionary' paranoia seized China, provoking a catalogue of atrocity. When this spread westwards, Kham and Amdo erupted into open warfare against the protagonists. Sixty thousand refugees fled into Tsang and the freedom fighters, under the command of Gompo Tashi, were increasing their numbers daily.

The resistance movement was becoming more effective but the Chinese showed no restraint in their methods. The PLA increased their strength to eight divisions. A force of 150,000 trained men with sophisticated battlefield technology now confronted an irregular band of horsemen and mountain warriors. As more villages and towns were destroyed, refugees began to descend on Lhasa.

The Khampa partisans did succeed in gaining control in a number of areas, preventing PLA movement. In autumn 1958, members of the *Chu-shi Gang-druk* besieged a major army encampment at the market town of Tsethang, south of the Brahmaputra river, just two days travel from Lhasa. Several thousand Chinese were killed but it was the last great victory of the brave Khampas. The Chinese commander in Lhasa, General Tan Kuan-sen demanded that the Dalai Lama mobilise the Tibetan Army against the rebels. He refused.

Early in 1959, the Chinese Governor invited the

Dalai Lama to watch a dance troupe from China perform in the military headquarters. Chiang Chin-wu's insistence that the invitation should remain secret and the sinister location for the event aroused the Tibetans' suspicions. On the appointed day in March a huge crowd of 30,000 gathered outside the *Norbulingka* (the Garden of Jewels) and prevented the Dalai Lama from leaving his summer palace.

Embittered refugees and thousands of monks who had come for the *Monlam Chenmo* prayer festival that takes place during Losar swelled the population of Lhasa. Intermingled amongst these people were some 6,000 armed Khampa rebels. The situation was volatile. There was a stand off for the next few days while the Chinese continued to demand that the Dalai Lama be taken to the military garrison for his own protection but the ever-increasing crowd refused to allow anyone in or out of the palace.

By now the Dalai Lama no longer had control over his own people, let alone the Chinese, and it was time for him to leave. On 17 March, a date deemed auspicious by the state oracle, concealed by one of Lhasa's dreaded sandstorms, the Dalai Lama, members of his family, his tutors, key ministers and attendants slipped away in disguise, crossed the Kyichu river in coracles, and headed for the mountains.

The party paused at Lhuntse *Dzong*, close to the border, where the Dalai Lama sent a letter to the Panchen Lama urging him to flee, but the message never got through. Then, after formally repudiating the

'Seventeen Point Agreement' and announcing the formation of his own government, the Dalai Lama and the 95 members of his party crossed into India.

Three days after the Dalai Lama left Lhasa the PLA shelled the Norbulingka, machine-gunning the defenceless crowd. Eight hundred Tibetans died trying to protect the palace, which they believed still contained their king. The Jokhang temple, which had been built in the 7th century and was Tibet's holiest shrine, and the Potala Palace were next to be bombarded. Thousands more Tibetans were to die before the guns fell silent and, after two days, when the revolt was finally crushed, corpses littered the streets.

On 28 March, the Tibetan Government was

Dalai Lama, members of his family, his tutors, key ministers and attendants fleeing Tibet on horseback.

dissolved; Tibet became a conquered territory. In a final act of repression, all the males in Lhasa between the ages of 16 and 60 were deported to China for forced labour.

The intrepid freedom fighters took to the hills to pursue their campaign of harassment against the PLA. But, over the next 18 months, a further 87,000 Tibetans were to die as a result of military action and all organised resistance within Tibet was effectively eradicated.

The Dalai Lama reached Assam on 30 March 1959, followed in subsequent months by 80,000 Tibetan refugees. Hundreds were to perish on the high Himalayan passes and many of those who made it to safety died of grief, shock or disease in the unfamiliar climate. The Dalai Lama first established his Government in Exile at Birla House in Mussoorie. In April 1960 he moved to his present seat at McLeod Ganj near Dharamsala.

Tsarong *Shappe* was arrested for helping the Dalai Lama to escape, and died in a Chinese military prison. The remnants of the *Chu-shi Gang-druk* militia withdrew to Mustang in Nepal from where they continued to mount undercover operations in Tibet until 1972.

Following the capitulation of Lhasa, Military Control Committees were established in all the major towns save Shigatse, which, under the control of the Panchen Lama, had remained peaceful. Thousands more Tibetans were arrested; guerrilla groups and those associated with the revolt were hunted down, and either executed on the spot or sent into slavery in China's *laogai* (labour camps).

Here conditions were a living hell. To give one example: of the 70,000 Tibetans imprisoned north of Langzhou, over half perished from starvation between 1959 and 1961. The monks of the great *gompas* were kept under guard in their assembly halls and then disbanded. Eventually the population of the monasteries and nunneries was reduced to just a few ageing caretakers.

Beijing now viewed the uprising as reason to abrogate all its pledges to Tibet under the 'Seventeen Point Agreement'; control of the population through 'strengthened administration' became their prime concern. First, the Tibet committee (PCART) was reformed to have jurisdiction over the former provinces of U and Tsang only; thus two-thirds of Tibet - the bulk of Kham and all of Amdo - was severed from the nation.

The new Tibet Autonomous Region (TAR), which was no longer autonomous, was divided up into seven districts, 72 counties and one municipality, Lhasa. Turning the focus of their patronage onto the Panchen Lama, they now made him the new Chairman of PCART.

Next, a programme of 'Democratic Reforms' was launched. A policy known as the 'Three Antis and Two Reductions' confiscated all property from nobles ('enemies of the people'), and began the systematic plunder of Tibet. The Potala, which contained the finest collection of Imperial Chinese art in the world and all the monasteries were stripped of their treasures. Sacred golden objects, such as gifts to former Dalai Lamas from neighbouring Emperors, were melted down into bullion and literally hundreds of tons of artefacts were shipped to China in convoys of trucks.

Then, 'Land Reform' was introduced, resulting in disastrous agricultural policies that caused widespread famine throughout China until 1963. Tens of thousands of Tibetans died of starvation as the majority of the Tibetan grain crop was shipped to the 'Motherland'.

Thamzing ('struggle sessions') became the scourge of daily life for Tibetan people. Citizens deemed in need of 'political education' were subjected to brutal public interrogations and, as a minimum punishment, were forced to endure humiliation in the streets constrained by a *gyangshing* (an agonising form of portable pillory). Failure to renounce family or religious loyalty would result in more terrible tortures or execution, and those sentenced to death had their tongues torn out with meat hooks to prevent them from shouting "Long live the Dalai Lama" before they died.

Burying alive, scalding, disembowelling and crucifixion were all practised and small children were even forced to shoot their own parents. Tibetans, who abhor the taking of life, had to kill their pet animals and adherence to any religious faith was outlawed.

The monasteries were ransacked and their inhabitants shamefully persecuted. In 1959, the monks from the Upper Tantric College in the Ramoche temple, Lhasa, were forced at gunpoint to break life-long vows of celibacy by publicly raping their nuns in front of the ruins of their establishment. By 1962, only eight of the 6,259 monasteries and nunneries in the whole of Tibet had escaped damage.

Choekyi Gyaltsen's relationship with the PRC

Throughout the life of the Tenth Panchen Lama, the Chinese attempted to use him to discredit the Dalai Lama and split Tibetan loyalties. Having been raised by the Chinese, Choekyi Gyaltsen was seen by many as 'Beijing's puppet' and a pretender for the post of spiritual leader but this ambiguous figure was in fact a devout and brave man, as will be shown.

At first, he maintained good relations with the PRC, and undertook a number of initiatives to promote the well being of the Tibetan people. But, as the extremism of communist policies unfolded, his disquiet increased, and he began to criticise the Beijing authorities openly.

Against the advice of his teacher, Ngulchu *Rinpoche*, the Panchen Lama denounced the atrocities committed by Chinese occupying forces, in a petition entitled: *Report on the suffering of the people of Tibet and Tibetan regions, and propositions for the future work of the Central Committee under the respectful supervision of Prime Minister Chou En-lai.*

This report, which became known as the *Seventy Thousand Characters*, was handed to Chou En-lai on 18 May 1962, and, during the next *Monlam Chenmo* prayer festival, the Panchen Lama declared his loyalty to Tenzin Gyatso, ending his address to the assembled crowd with the words "Long live the Dalai Lama".

The Communists immediately accused him of anti-Chinese and Counter-Revolutionary activities and dismissed him from his duties. He was arrested and subjected to numerous *thamzing* sessions of public criticism, particularly in 1966 at the National Institute of Minorities.

Mao described the *Seventy Thousand Characters* as "a poisoned arrow shot at the Party" and its author "a reactionary feudal overlord". The Panchen Lama refused to repent and was taken to Qincheng jail in Beijing, where he spent the next ten years in solitary confinement. It is reported that he repeatedly tried to starve himself. The Panchen's loyal tutor, Ngulchu Lobsang Choephel, was also imprisoned and, subsequently, beaten to death.

Concerned about the number of people fleeing abroad, Beijing temporarily reined back on its persecution of Tibetans in 1963, imposing some restrictions on arrests and allowing some freedoms. In the early 1960s, China's President, Liu Shaoqi, had adopted a more moderate line following the debacle of the 'Great Leap Forward', but in June 1966, Mao Tse-tung was returned to power with the help of the army. In August, he announced the Cultural Revolution to "cleanse China of its rotten core".

The Cultural Revolution

> *Do not mourn, people of Tibet,*
> *Independence will surely be ours.*
> *Remember our sun,*
> *Remember His Holiness.*

(A Tibetan underground song during the Cultural Revolution)

Whilst the rape of Tibet prior to the Cultural Revolution

had been organised, now Mao's adolescent Red Guards invoked mob rule and wanton destruction ensued throughout China. In Tibet hundreds of priceless frescoes and images, dating back to the time of Songtsen Gampo were defaced, and the remaining stockpiles of treasure, stored for shipment to China, were smashed. Tibetans were forced to demolish their palaces and monasteries and giant bonfires were lit to burn the ancient scriptures.

The Red Guards made a public display of the destruction of a special collection of illuminated manuscripts housed in the Potala. Nothing symbolised the 'Four Olds' better than these 2,000 sacred volumes exquisitely written in inks made from powdered gold, silver and precious stones on ancient palm leaves brought from India a thousand years before. Those religious texts not incinerated were desecrated by being used as lavatory paper in the Chinese latrines.

Under Martial Law, everything Tibetan was destroyed; everything Communist Chinese, adopted. Even the Tibetans' love of flowers was disallowed. The drab replaced the cheerful and colourful. All Tibetans were forced to study the teachings of Mao Tse-tung; religious practice, wearing traditional costumes or showing a Tibetan flag would result in arrest and brutal sessions of *thamzing*, often followed by death.

A coalition of Red Guard groups formed the 'Great Alliance', which embarked upon a campaign to prove itself more Maoist than rival factions. This led to open warfare against the 'Revolutionary Rebels' in the streets of Lhasa and the fighting spread to Shigatse, Gyantse and elsewhere. Hundreds died from mutilation and torture and the country dissolved into total chaos.

In September 1968, a Cultural Revolution Committee was formed in Tibet, which brought the Red Guards under Beijing's control for the first time, and some semblance of relative order returned.

Early in 1969 a large-scale revolt took place in several different parts of Tibet. The reprisals that followed are said to have exceeded those of the 1959 uprising, but little is known of the true facts as knowledge of the event could only be gleaned by word of mouth from escaping refugees.

Fighting eventually ceased at the end of that year but, although the anarchy of the Cultural Revolution finished, its political aftermath lasted another seven years, until the death of Mao in 1976. As a consequence of the tyranny of 'The Great Helmsman', Tibet was now a broken, poverty-ridden police state in which the land, its people, and even its captors, all suffered from a pervasive loss of will. In all, over one million Tibetans, a fifth of the population, had died as a result of Chinese occupation up until the end of the Cultural Revolution.

The final years of the Panchen Lama

Chou En-lai tried to have the Panchen Lama freed in 1974, but he himself came under attack from the Gang of Four. It was not until Chou and Mao were both dead and the Gang of Four had fallen that the Panchen Lama was finally released on 10 October 1977. It was a further eleven years before his designation as an 'anti Party element' was revoked.

However it seemed that the authorities were now able to manipulate him once again. During his first public appearance in 14 years, he urged the Dalai Lama to return to Tibet, proclaiming an improvement in conditions there under Chinese rule. Then came an extraordinary development that outraged devout Tibetans. The Panchen Lama married Li Jie, a former PLA doctor and the daughter of a Kuomintang general, in 1978. Later they were to have a daughter.

In 1979 he was appointed vice-chairman of both the Chinese People's Political Consultative Conference and the National People's Congress. In 1982 he was allowed to leave Beijing for the first time and travelled extensively in Amdo and Kham to promote good Tibetan/Chinese relations. When he returned to Lhasa for a brief visit that year, despite his inappropriate marriage, he was feted by thousands of Tibetans. This overwhelming display of devotion shocked Beijing.

The brave yet wayward lama remained provocative to the end. As he made offerings in the Tsuglagkhang temple and prostrated himself before the statue of Jowo *Rinpoche* he prayed for the Dalai Lama's return, whispering audibly: "There is but one man who is worthy to sit on this throne – His Holiness Tenzin Gyatso". On hearing these words, the temple guards fled for fear of Chinese reprisals.

He again expounded his friendship for the Dalai Lama at the 1985 *Monlam Chenmo*. In March 1987, in a speech given to the Tibetan Autonomous Region Standing Committee of the National People's Congress in Beijing, he reiterated many of the points in his *Seventy Thousand Characters* report.

Then, during a rare visit to Tibet in 1989, when presiding over the consecration of the renovated Fourth Panchen Lama's *stupa* at Tashilhunpo (which had been previously damaged by the Red Guards), Choekyi Gyaltsen declared that Chinese occupation of Tibet had brought more destruction than benefit to the Tibetan people.

Four days later, on 28 January, the Panchen Lama unexpectedly died of a 'heart attack'. He was only 51.

His body was embalmed and, when the Tashilhunpo monks went to pay their respects: they noticed that his

Chinese troops beneath the Potala Palace, Lhasa, 1989

flesh had turned black, giving credence to the theory of foul play - most Tibetans believing he had been poisoned on the orders of Beijing.

Following his death, hundreds of students protested against Chinese occupation; in March 1989, a three-day demonstration in Lhasa was put down by troops. Over a hundred Tibetans were killed and Martial Law was declared.

Three months later, the PLA massacred followers of the Democracy Movement in Tiananmen Square.

5

The 11th Panchen Lama

The search for the reincarnation and the contest for primacy

Shortly after the Tenth Panchen Lama died, Beijing appointed the Abbot of Tashilhunpo, Chadrel *Rinpoche*, a lama trusted by the PRC for his loyalty to the Communist Party, to lead the committee responsible for identifying his reincarnation. To give the impression of concern for religious affairs, the Chinese also provided a generous grant to fund the construction of a *stupa* for Choekyi Gyaltsen's remains. Chadrel passed word that he wished the Dalai Lama to pray for a speedy discovery.

In 1992, the Chinese did not object to Tenzin Gyatso's role in the choice of the 17th Karmapa – the 'Black Hat' Lama. No process of lottery was used to aid the selection of this important sub-sect leader. The Dalai Lama, who had dreamt about the location of the boy's birthplace, gave his blessing to the enthronement of the

Chadrel Rinpoche

six-year-old Urgyen Trinley Dorje at the Tsurphu monastery in Tibet.

Believing he would now be included in the search for the next Panchen, the Dalai Lama asked permission to send a delegation of his own monks to observe prophetic visions at the sacred lake, Lhamo Lhatso. This request was refused, the Chinese Government saying there was no need for 'outside interference'. In an attempt to maintain this facade of non-intervention, they added that the matter was in the hands of the Tashilhunpo search committee.

In July 1993, the Chinese Government did allow a direct meeting between Chadrel and the Dalai Lama's representative, his brother, Gyalo Thondup. After some initial obstruction, they met in a hotel in Beijing under the watchful eye of a Tibetan-speaking Chinese official.

Chadrel said that he did want contact with the Dalai Lama, and passed over a letter and offerings to take to Dharamsala. He was, however, silent on the matter of access to the sacred lake. Gayalo Thondrup then took the issue of the Dalai Lama's involvement to Hu Jintao, a former TAR party secretary and future Politburo member.

The delegation returned to India and, suitably encouraged, the Dalai Lama hastily issued an invitation for Chadrel to visit him in Dharamsala. There was no reply. In September the Chinese Ambassador in Delhi gave a belligerent speech on Tibet and it appeared the optimism had been misplaced. The PRC, feeling their authority was being undermined, now took a stronger line.

The Chinese premier, Li Peng, declared, "strangers would not be allowed to interfere", and made public the five stages that the process of selection was to follow:

1. The consultation of mystical signs to determine candidates.

2. The setting of tradition tests.

3. The use of oracles and divination.

4. The drawing of lots by a Chinese official (use of the Golden Urn).

5. Final approval by Beijing authorities.

The first three stages conformed to religious tradition, but the last two were Chinese requirements not recognised by Tibetans.

The Communists also claimed that, just prior to his death, Choekyi Gyaltsen had instructed a gathering of high-ranking lamas to select his successor by drawing lots from the Golden Urn in front of the statue of *Shakyamuni* in the Jokhang temple (the use of the Golden Urn referring back to Emperor Qianlong's request of 1792). However, to suit their purposes, the Chinese were quoting the Panchen Lama out of context. He had been referring to *takril*, the Tibetan practice of rolling dough balls to determine reincarnations of lamas.

In the January 1988 issue of 'China Reconstructs', the Tenth Panchen Lama wrote of the need for his own and the Dalai Lama's reincarnations to be mutually recognised. Now, a year after his death, posters appeared on the walls of the Drepung monastery in Lhasa challenging Chinese authority over the search for the Panchen's *tulku*, and endorsing the requirement for the Dalai Lama to approve the nominee.

Between December 1990 and July 1993, monks in all the Tibetan monasteries daily recited sacred texts to aid the search. A delegation of lamas, overseen by Zhao Puchu, the chairman of the Buddhist Association of China, performed ceremonies at Lhamo Lhatso. Taking the direction that the Panchen Lama had faced when he died and the secrets revealed by the 'lake of visions', the search area was narrowed down to a region east of Tashilhunpo.

The priests reconvened at the monastery to recite more prayers beside the embalmed body of the Panchen, and to listen to the trances of the Nechung and Tsangpa *kuden*. The oracles' gesticulations, hissing, groaning and unintelligible mouthings were interpreted by their secretaries and, thus guided, the lamas sent out search parties to scour the countryside.

Unknown at the time, the Beijing authorities held a top-level meeting, the Third Forum on Tibet, in July 1994. It was addressed by Jiang Zemin, who was being groomed as successor to the failing patriarch Deng Xiaoping.

The outcome of this meeting was a hardening of the Chinese position over the troublesome religious community, concluding that, rather than rapprochement with the Dalai Lama, the total removal of his influence was the better option. The conflict between Dharamsala and Beijing was now to take a more dangerous course.

Chadrel *Rinpoche* sent a message to the Dalai Lama to tell him of signs at the lake that indicated the lama had been reincarnated. Tenzin Gyatso wrote to the Chinese authorities, via their embassy in Delhi, to stress the importance of his involvement. He invited the search committee to India for consultations. Beijing, which now suspected there was a secret channel of communication between the Dalai Lama and Chadrel, described these 'manoeuvres' as an attempt to "influence traitors who wished to split the Motherland" and declined to answer.

During 1994 there were 28 children, whose date

and place of birth fitted the clues, identified as potential reincarnations. The lamas returned to the lake in October for more divine inspiration. Eventually the list was refined to just eight candidates, including two born outside Tibet, in Ladakh and Dharamsala. Armed with more clues from the visions, one indicating a strange mark on the body of the reincarnate, the search was resumed.

Chadrel entrusted the highly respected monk and incarnate lama, Ngagchen *Rinpoche*, with the task of visiting the eight candidates. In the region of Nagchu, he found a five-year-old boy who made a deep impression on him; in fact, Ngagchen was never to lose the conviction that this was the child for whom they had been searching. When the lama asked him where he came from the boy replied, "I come from Tashilhunpo".

Amongst other good signs, a mark was found on his body that complied with the vision. Ngagchen also reported that the boy's wrists showed evidence of the handcuffs that had been used on the late Panchen Lama. The boy attached himself to the strange monk and tried to accompany him when he left. This behaviour was commonly recognised as the will of a reincarnate to resume his religious life. The lengthy process of identifying the Panchen's *tulku* was nearing conclusion, but the political side was still to be resolved.

The Chinese were impatient for a decision by the following March; time was running out if the use of the Urn was to be avoided. The Dalai Lama was hoping that he could meet Chadrel in person during the Kalachakra initiation – one of the most important teachings in Tibetan Buddhism – which was due to take place in Mundgod, southern India, shortly after New Year. He was also under pressure from Tashilhunpo's mirror monastery near Bylakuppe, in the far south of India, to arrange for the Panchen's *tulku* to be brought out of Tibet once he had been found.

Chadrel could not get permission to travel to India himself, but he did find a way of getting information the Dalai Lama needed passed on to him. When the Dalai Lama arrived in Mundgod in January 1995 a mysterious monk handed him a package. It was a complete list of all the candidates, more than 20 photographs and a long letter from Chadrel explaining the evidence of each case. There was also a proposal as to how matters should proceed. Chadrel maintained that the Dalai Lama must make the final selection but he insisted that the boy be allowed to take up his historic residence in the Tashilhunpo monastery of Tibet, not India.

His plan involved an innocent subterfuge: the Dalai Lama would identify the child and convey the name to Chadrel. Then, having ensured that the Dalai Lama's candidate emerged as the choice of the search committee, Chadrel would present his findings to the Chinese, and persuade them to approve the selection without using the Golden Urn.

Once all the formalities were complete, and the boy had been enthroned at Tashilhunpo, the Dalai Lama could declare his involvement. The Chinese would be angry at the deception, but it would be too late for them

Tashilhunpo monastery in Tibet, the historic residence of the Panchen Lama

to renege on their recognition of the child.

It was a clever if risky plot. The flaw, as the Dalai Lama saw it, was that if he delayed his announcement until after the Chinese had made theirs, the community in exile and his followers in Tibet would perceive him to be a puppet of Beijing. Despite this, he agreed to go along with Chadrel's plan for the time being and, once recognised, the Panchen should take his traditional seat in Tibet.

The Dalai Lama then put himself into isolation to consider his choice. First he conducted divinations each day to determine when he should make his decision. Two days later, on Wednesday 25 January, the dice deemed it auspicious for him to proceed. After many hours of special meditations and further divinations, he had his answer. It was the boy from Nagchu who had been favoured by Ngagchen *Rinpoche*. His name was Choekyi Nyima.

The following day the monk messenger set off in haste for Tibet. The journey should have taken four days, but snow blocked the passes on the Nepalese frontier and so it was not until 10 February that the breathless envoy arrived in Shigatse.

The news had come too late for an important meeting of the search committee and, although the Tashilhunpo group favoured the boy from Nagchu, some of the other committee members wanted to resolve the issue by lottery.

Chadrel now resorted to deception and claimed that he had performed a divination that had singled out Choekyi Nyima as the true reincarnate. He informed the authorities of the choice but the search committee, with its Chinese placemen, Sengchen Lobsang Gyaltsen and Sandrup, the local party secretary, refused to accept it. Undeterred, Chadrel set off for Beijing.

His visit coincided with the National People's Congress. On 4 March Chadrel attended the National Political Consultative Committee's third meeting. He had a number of items associated with the Panchen's death to resolve. One was payment for the *stupa* at Tashilhunpo; another was the difficult matter of the Panchen's wife, who disputed the disposal of his considerable assets. Although Li Jie was a Buddhist, she chose the more conventional Chinese interpretation of inheritance rather than the Tibetan one, which deems a lama's wealth should pass to his reincarnation.

Lastly he addressed the issue of the search for the Panchen's successor. Chadrel explained that a boy had been selected from the shortlist by divination so there was no need for use of the Golden Urn. But by now the Chinese distrusted him and summoned eleven members of the search committee to Beijing.

Sengchen, a hard-line lay politician who was hated by the Tashilhunpo camp, led the argument against the selection of Choekyi Nyima and won over the Chinese.

Chadrel appeared before the State Council, in the presence of both Li Peng and Jiang Zemin, to plead his case. His impulsiveness was seen as proof of collusion, and he was confined in his quarters in Beijing. He was never to return to Tashilhunpo.

Meanwhile, the Dalai Lama, who had heard nothing from Tibet for six weeks, was getting desperate. He feared that the Chinese would make their selection from the Golden Urn and announce the result on 23 May, the anniversary of the signing of the Seventeen Point Agreement. The only way to prevent that was to announce first.

The next auspicious date was the anniversary of the birth of Buddha on the full moon of 14 May. He resolved to seek Chadrel's approval of his intention to declare his hand. But, unbeknown to Dharamsala, Chadrel was being held in China, and all attempts to contact him appeared fruitless. In fact Chadrel did get the message but his reply, which pleaded for a delay, never got returned. With no news, on the eve of the 14th, the Dalai Lama cast a divination and consulted the oracle to determine whether the time was right to make his announcement. The answer came back that it was.

The following morning, after hours of meditation and prayer, the Dalai Lama made his way to the Hall of Ceremonies where a collection of dignitaries and prominent lamas had been hastily assembled to receive him. Seated cross-legged on his throne, he read a simple prayer that he had written for the occasion. It was a prayer for the long life of Gedhun Choekyi Nyima, a six-year-old boy from the village of Lhari in the province of Nagchu, whom he had selected as the reincarnation of the Tenth Panchen Lama. He announced that he had given the boy his religious name, Tenzin Gedhun Yeshe Thrinley Phuntsog Pal Sangpo, and asked Tibetans everywhere to pray for the boy. The following is an extract of his address to the congregation in Dharamsala:

"Unable to influence the search with my own delegation, I received the names and details of the candidates and the auspicious signs concerning them. Following offerings and prayers before the images of Buddha and the thangka of Palden Lhamo I did a mo [dice divination] while uttering the children's names to find the more likely candidates. I then rolled the dough balls with the names hidden within, and on each test the same one emerged, jumping out on its own as if by magic."

The Dalai Lama had faced an impossible dichotomy. Taking the religious priority, he had acted to ensure that the genuine reincarnation of the Panchen Lama was selected. But it was not a diplomatic move and what was to follow caused him terrible anguish.

The aftermath of the Dalai Lama's announcement

While all Tibet celebrated the happy news of the new *tulku*, the Chinese were incensed that they had been duped. Beijing reacted without delay, and launched an intensive political campaign against the Dalai Lama. On 17 May 1995, the Chinese arrested Chadrel *Rinpoche* and his secretary, Jampa Chung, who were in Chengdu at the time.

Whilst under interrogation in custody, Chadrel was put under enormous pressure to renounce the Dalai Lama and reject his choice of Panchen but he refused to submit. Then all contact was lost; those who enquired of his whereabouts were told that he was ill.

Next the Chinese moved in on Lhari, the home of the child recognised as the Panchen Lama. Choekyi Nyima; his father, Konchok Phuntsog, a doctor in the local hospital; his mother, Dechen Chodon, a nurse, and his elder brother were taken away. They have not been seen since.

Five thousand PLA troops were transferred to Shigatse, and a 're-education work team' of 50 Party officials was sent to the monastery. All those associated with the circle of Chadrel were interrogated and Jampa

Chung was brought back to Tashilhunpo to 'confess' in front of the lamas that 'incorrect policy' had been followed during the search for the Panchen.

The monks, led by Ngagchen *Rinpoche*, resisted. They refused to deny that the true Panchen had been found and adopted a policy of non-co-operation. On the night of 12 July security forces, backed by the PLA, broke into the monastery and put down the protest by force. Fifty-six of the resident monks, bound and bleeding, were driven away in trucks. For the remainder, *thamzing* sessions, beatings and torture with electric shocks became their daily lot until they confessed their errors.

The monks were told that anyone in possession of a photograph of Choekyi Nyima, or the Dalai Lama's long-life prayer for him, would be shot. At least one monk committed suicide rather than betray his beliefs. As news of the revolt spread to Lhasa, posters appeared denouncing Chinese interference in the selection process.

Tashilhunpo was closed to the public, and Chadrel's enemy in the search committee, Sengchen Lobsang Gyaltsen, was returned to leadership of the monastery; a post he had held as a ruthless exponent of the Red Guards during the Cultural Revolution. In a public statement he denounced the appointment of the *tulku* as a fraudulent trick, claiming that the Dalai Lama had not only acted illegally by not fulfilling all five stages of the selection process but had also blasphemed the wishes of the last Panchen.

He further declared that Choekyi Nyima's parents were bad people who had lied about their son's date of birth, and that the boy had once drowned a dog: "a heinous crime in the eyes of Buddha". Early in 1996 a bomb was detonated at Sengchen's house in Lhasa, but there were no casualties.

In August 1995, a delegation of handpicked Tibetans, half made up of senior lamas, was summoned to a conference in Beijing. They were housed in the Jingxi guest-house, which was guarded by its proprietors, the PLA, and forced under the threat of punishment to reject the Dalai Lama's choice of Panchen. They were then paraded in front of the Press, and a photograph of the 75 meek Tibetans standing with Jiang Zemin in the Great Hall of the People appeared in all the newspapers.

On 11 October, the Dalai Lama wrote to Jiang Zemin to express concern for the missing boy lama and the need for his proper religious upbringing. He said he regretted the strain upon their relations but explained that his actions were motivated purely by religious tradition.

The selection of China's candidate

The Chinese now made their move to provide a replacement for Choekyi Nyima. Having apparently dispensed with the first three stages of the process, they put up three candidates for selection by lottery. The date was set for 29 November 1995 and several hundreds of heavily armed soldiers were positioned strategically around the capital to prevent access to the Jokhang temple as the delegates arrived from Beijing.

After an opening speech by the Governor of the Autonomous Region of Tibet, three ivory tablets with the names of the candidates were shown to representatives of the State Council. These were then sealed in silk bags and put in the Golden Urn. The urn was placed in front of the statue of *Shakyamuni* to the accompaniment of much chanting, and Pomi Jampa Lodrop, the chairman of the Tibetan branch of the Buddhist Association, drew out one bag.

Pomi Jampa Lodrop, the chairman of the Tibetan branch of the Buddhist Association, draws a bag out of the Golden Urn

He then announced: "Fate has decreed that it is Gyantsen Norbu". Eyewitnesses later reported that one of the tablets was larger than the others, and could easily have been identified by touch. The sham was revealed as the boy appeared immediately from behind a red curtain already attired in the ceremonial costume of a lama. Both Norbu's parents had been members of the Communist Party since 1977 and his selection had clearly been rigged. This absurd masquerade ended in forced jubilation.

A film of the ceremony, featuring prominent participation by Chinese officials, was shown on television in Lhasa for the next six weeks and thousands of photographs of the boy were circulated for display throughout Tibet - a practice formerly forbidden by the Chinese.

Setting aside the emotional aspects of this disturbing outcome, anomalies in the behaviour of both sides made controversy inevitable.

When, in 1992, the Chinese involved the exiled Kagyu lamas and the Dalai Lama in the selection of the 17th Karmapa Lama, they made no demands for use of the Golden Urn. In the early stages of the search for the 11th Panchen Lama they had been content for the Dalai Lama to consult with Tashilhunpo. Then there was a dramatic change in policy. But by their brutal reaction to the Dalai Lama's announcement, the Chinese have attracted the unwelcome attention of the outside world.

On the other hand, Tenzin Gyatso's public seizure of authority over the selection process, mirroring the behaviour of the Kuomintang in 1949, was bound to infuriate the Chinese and set back any hope of improving relations with them in the near future. His insistence that his only concern was correct religious practice was unlikely to be believed by the Chinese. To them, his use of the dough balls indicated that a form of lottery, albeit traditionally Tibetan, was acceptable, and that politics, rather than methodology, was the issue.

6

The victims of the controversy

This episode drew together all the strands of modern Chinese paranoia - interpretation of history, religious authority and Tibetan nationalism - into a single, volatile contest of wills. The need to save face had an immediate consequence for the two young boys and their families, but the ultimate victim is Tibet itself.

Chadrel Rinpoche

Chadrel *Rinpoche*'s former loyalty to the PRC made his actions all the more treacherous in Chinese eyes and they needed to set an example to discourage other lama 'double agents'. Despite two years of interrogation and coercion, Chadrel remained true to a promise he had made to the Dalai Lama and never denied his support for Gedhun Choekyi Nyima. In May 1997, the Xinhua news agency reported that Chadrel had been tried and found guilty of "leaking state secrets, conspiring to split the country and colluding with separatist forces abroad". He was sentenced to six years' imprisonment and three years' deprivation of political rights.

Jampa Chung, his secretary, was found guilty on the same charges but was given a lesser sentence. Shortly after this announcement, it was established that Chadrel was in solitary confinement in Chuandong Number 3 Prison in Sichuan province. He was reported to be on hunger strike and in very poor health. In March 2002, during the EU/China dialogue being held in Madrid, the Chinese authorities announced that Chadrel Rinpoche had been released. There was no word on the whereabouts of the 62-year-old or the state of his health.

Gedhun Choekyi Nyima

After the abduction of Choekyi Nyima and his family, the issue became a focus of international interest and concern and the Chinese government had to give a response. The Foreign Ministry spokesman, Shen Guofang, said that the boy was neither missing nor reincarnated and should be wherever he was born. However Amnesty International had obtained reports from Lhari that none of the family had been seen there since May 1995.

In May 1996, the Chinese authorities finally admitted that they had placed the boy under their protection to prevent his kidnap by separatists. It was believed that he was being held in Beijing but there was no news of his family.

The victims of the controversy

Mary Robinson, the UN High Commissioner for Human Rights, was denied her request to see him during a visit to Beijing in 1998. The Chinese also refused a plea for access made at the Human Rights talks held in Washington. Nothing further was heard until a mysterious article appeared on the Internet in November 1999.

In this, Ma Chongliang, the Gansu reporter for the China Freedom News Association, described sinister events that took place at Lanzhou Prison Number 1 in Gansu on 19 October 1999.

Quoting an eyewitness, he wrote that a special squad of 'Han Fighters', selected for their political reliability by the Gansu People's Armed Police, were instructed to take an unmarked vehicle and convey the corpse of a major criminal from the jail to the crematorium under armed escort. During the transit to the suburbs of Lanzhou they discovered the body to be one of a young, emaciated boy. When shown a photograph of Choekyi Nyima, the witness confirmed that it could have been the same person.

It is not inconceivable that Choekyi Nyima was being held in the province of Gansu, which is a remote area mainly closed to tourists, but the identification of this boy's corpse is based on thin hearsay evidence. There are also some doubts over the source of the report. But, if the incident took place, the measures taken to ensure secrecy are indicative of the importance of this dead prisoner.

Two years later, on 29 October 2001, Chinese

officials told an Australian human rights delegation that Choekyi Nyima was fine but his parents did not want him to be bothered. However, all attempts to arrange access to the boy by an independent mediator in order that the Chinese claims can be verified have been met with persistent resistance.

Gyantsen Norbu

On 8 December 1995, Gyantsen Norbu was formally enthroned at Tashilhunpo in a carefully stage-managed ceremony. Agents of the Public Security Bureau, the Chinese equivalent of the former Soviet Union's KGB, manned the entrance and checked the identities of the specially selected witnesses. Five hundred soldiers were stationed throughout the monastery to quell any disturbance. The ceremony was condemned by the *Kashag* in Dharamsala as invalid and against the wishes of the Tibetan people.

Despite being spoilt by the authorities (within weeks of being appointed he was presented with a luxury limousine), the five-year-old Norbu is also a victim of this tragedy.

Spirited away to China for his 'own protection', he has received intensive religious instruction under the tutelage of Bomi *Rinpoche*, the acting *Ganden tripa*. But he has little freedom as he has been confined in a villa in Huairou County, on the outskirts of Beijing, and is guarded day and night by the PLA. Here he remains in obscurity, except on the few occasions that his masters choose to impose his popularity upon the Tibetan

Gyantsen Norbu, the boy who the Chinese recognise as Panchen Lama, is also a victim of this tragedy

people or use him for political ends.

In February 1997, the Chinese state-run news agency, Xinhua, reported the boy's grief at the passing of Deng Xiaoping. In a charm offensive the following year, it was announced that he had donated 30,000 yuan to snowstorm victims in Nagchu and was now able to recite 4,000 pages of Buddhist text.

In early 1998, the Chinese government, believing they had now eradicated any opposition to Norbu, ordered the Abbot of Kumbum monastery, Agya *Rinpoche*, to make a permanent home for the boy in

Amdo. Despite being a prominent political figure as Vice President of the Buddhist Association of China, Agya refused. When the Chinese tried to force him he left the country (he now lives in California). To the embarrasment of the authorities, a second of Beijing's apparently compliant senior lamas had been prepared to forfeit everything rather than collaborate over the Panchen Lama dispute.

In 1999, Gyantsen Norbu returned to Tibet for the first time since his enthronement. Amidst unprecedented security, he was whisked from the airport to Lhasa under cover of darkness, and began a three-day programme of religious fixtures at the Jokhang temple on 17 June.

Next, he travelled to Shigatse in a 21-vehicle motorcade. On arrival at Tashilhunpo, an honour guard of 600 lamas greeted him. Surrounded by agents with walkie-talkies, he then officiated at the annual *thangka* ceremony where a 100-foot satin depiction of 'The Buddha of Today' is unfurled.

Several thousand pilgrims came to witness the event and receive blessings but monks were warned that they would be sacked from the monastery if they did not show due respect for the Chinese Panchen. One elderly lama stated, with a deadpan expression, that he felt "unlimited happiness" at the boy's arrival.

Xinhua coverage of the event included numerous references to the validity of Norbu's selection process, along with yet more superlatives to describe the boy's religious potential. It was now claimed that his birth was accompanied by some astonishing visions. However the report of a peacock nesting on the roof of his house is fanciful, even for Tibetan imagination, and his mother's recollection of the religious signs she found on Norbu's body when he was a baby is a somewhat incongruous memory for an atheist Party member.

Shortly after his return to Beijing, on 27 June, the China News Digest quoted Norbu exhorting other lamas and true believers "to follow the instructions of President Jiang Zemin, love the Communist Party of China, love our socialist Motherland, and love the religion we believe in".

In February 2000 he appeared on Chinese state-run television to express his "deep regard for the great family of the Motherland and the Chinese Communist Party's correct policies on religion." A recent Press release quoted a leading party official, Wang Zhoaguo, as saying "the boy was now concentrating on his study of *sutra* to become a patriotic living Buddha."

By controlling the office of Panchen Lama, the PRC is continuing a strategy practised by the Imperialists in 1910 and the Nationalists in 1923: manipulation of its latest puppet is clearly in full swing. The best that can be hoped for is that, one-day, Norbu will show the independent spirit of his predecessor and regain the trust of the Tibetan people.

Consequences for Tibet

The Chinese are playing a long game in advance of the Dalai Lama's death. On 17 January 2000 the two-year-old Sonam Puncog was selected as the Seventh Reting

Rinpoche. This office has a precedent for appointment as Regent. The Fifth Reting Lama was instrumental in the search for Tenzin Gyatso.

Having already established the child Panchen under their wing, this was a strategic move to influence the upbringing of another *tulku* who will endorse their choice of Dalai Lama in due course. However, if China enthrones a false reincarnation of His Holiness, one selected by lamas whom Tibetans believe to be impostors, they will risk inciting revolt throughout the entire Buddhist community.

While Tenzin Gyatso remains an anathema to the PRC, his insistence upon non-violence provides a check on the behaviour of his people. It would be greatly in the Chinese interest to understand that allowing the selection of a credible religious leader, without manipulation, would provide the most effective safeguard for peace and stability in the region and reconciliation with the present Dalai Lama would be an act of wise diplomacy.

7

Tibet today

China's latest policy on religion

The 1998 White Paper on human rights in Tibet
stipulates freedom of religious belief and the Chinese
refer to Tibetan Buddhism (*Zangchuan fojiao*) as a
distinct religious tradition. Under Chinese law, officials
who deprive citizens of this freedom of belief can be
imprisoned for up to two years. Although a front of
apparent respectability is presented, in reality the PRC
does not practise tolerance. While content to exploit
aspects of religion, such as the Buddhist concept of
reincarnation, for political ends, Communists consider
'The Party' to be the only guidance required in life; any
other loyalty is a rival to this ideology.

It was this doctrine that led to Soviet repression of
Buddhism in Outer Mongolia. In 1937, Stalin ordered
the destruction of monasteries; 20,000 lamas were
executed and a further 80,000 were deported to the

camps in Siberia, never to return.

The Cultural Revolution, which devastated all of China, had failed as a political initiative. When, during the 1980s, the Chinese authorities began to realise the significance of religion in Tibet, they exercised less brutality towards the lamas. Some of the better known monasteries were restored, national dress could be worn again and, for the first time in 20 years, elderly Tibetans were permitted to circumambulate the Jokhang temple and the *Lingkhor*. Heinrich Harrer was guardedly optimistic about Tibet's future after his return to Lhasa in 1982.

But this thaw in relations was to last just four years, ending irrevocably in 1989 with 'Tiananmen Square', after which the executions and torture recommenced. The short period of tolerance had merely been *dzuma* (sham) - a ruse "to allow the poison to show itself so that it could be lanced once and for all".

The PRC cannot separate anything from politics and at the heart of its policy is a perception that religion is linked to pro-democracy and independence movements. In 1994, Beijing's Third Forum on Work in Tibet announced:

> *"We must teach and guide Tibetan Buddhism to reform itself. All those religious laws and rituals must be reformed in order to fit in with the needs of development and stability in Tibet and they should be reformed so that they become appropriate to a society under socialism. The struggle between ourselves and*

the Dalai clique is neither a matter of religious belief, nor a matter of the question of autonomy, it is a matter of securing the unity of our country and opposing splittism".

They formalised this policy in 1996 with the 'Strike Hard' campaign, which was launched throughout China. It invoked tight control over the Tibetan monasteries and nunneries by appointing Democratic Management Committees to oversee the intensive 're-education' of their inhabitants. Under a political oath, all monks and nuns had to oppose the idea of an independent Tibet and denounce the Dalai Lama.

In May 1996, the monks of the Ganden monastery refused to comply with the embargo on photographs of the Dalai Lama. The security forces moved in, shot three of the protagonists, and carried away 86 others under arrest.

Failure to comply with the PRC's recent policy of religious containment in Tibet has resulted in 1,293 arrests, of whom 29 were executed. All told, 10,569 monks and nuns have been forced to leave their establishments. Over a third of those expelled are children, who are no longer allowed to join the monasteries whilst under 18.

The majority of *gompas* have now been closed down, only a few remaining as functioning entities, primarily to provide an impression of normality to visitors from the West. The great monastic universities of Ganden, Drepung and Sera are mere shadows of what they once were.

Tibet today

The force behind such ruthless execution of policy was the last Communist Party Secretary of the Autonomous Region, Chen Kuiyuan, who was transferred from Inner Mongolia, where he impressed Beijing with his efficiency. He was so unpopular in Tibet that he chose to live in Chengdu, the provincial capital of Sichuan, rather than Lhasa. Recently he declared that Tibet is a non-Buddhist region.

The latest crackdown on religious activities by the authorities in Lhasa is the most severe and wide ranging of recent years. It is being referred to as 'The Second Cultural Revolution'.

An announcement in the *Tibet Daily* on 4 July 2000 instructed parents and teachers to educate their children in atheism *"... in order to help rid them of the bad influence of religion"*. A new media network has been created to promulgate the Central Government's instructions, one of which barred school students from visiting the monasteries and temples to pray or attend religious ceremonies during the summer holidays.

Youngsters are told that Tibetan Buddhist practice is 'backward behaviour' and an obstacle to progress. Many children have been given detention or forced to pay fines when they have failed to observe the ban on wearing *srung mdud* (traditional Buddhist protection cords) and, in some cases these have been torn from the child, cut to pieces, and burnt in front of the class.

In September 2000, red banners denouncing the Dalai Lama were displayed outside the university. Possession of *thangkas* (religious paintings) has been declared illegal and security personnel have been instructed to search private houses for shrines and, particularly, photographs of the Dalai Lama. Discovery of any forbidden item incurs a fine of several hundred yuan and the confiscated objects are thrown into the Tsangpo River.

The most recent measure against the religious community has been the expulsion of students from the Serthar Buddhist Institute in Kham and the arrest of its founder, Khenpo Jigme Phuntsok. Over 1,000 dwellings close to the Institute were destroyed during October and November 2001.

The 'road to socialism' prescribed by the Chinese calls for a complete transformation of the Tibetan way of life. But, throughout 50 years of brutal occupation, efforts to shake the inherent beliefs of the Tibetan people have proved a total failure.

One reason for this is the sanctity of the land itself. The monasteries might lie in ruins, but the Chinese cannot destroy Tibet's sacred lakes and mountains, which are also the temples of its people.

The four great rivers of the Indian subcontinent - the Indus, Sutlej, Ganges and Brahmaputra – all originate at the base of Mount Kailash in Tibet. This is the most sacred peak in all Asia, revered by Hindus, Buddhists and Bonpo as the home of their gods.

Apart from the 11th century Tibetan poet, Milarepa, who is said to have been carried to the peak of Mount Kailash on a ray of sunlight, no one has climbed the mountain.

Recent Chinese permission for a Spanish team to attempt an assault on the 6,714-metre peak caused great offence to both Hindus and Buddhists and indicates the PRC's contempt for religious sensitivity. However this decision has subsequently been reversed following the widespread criticism from not just religious spokesmen, but also world governments and climbing organisations.

In the lull following the passing of Mao and the Gang of Four, Teng Hsiao-ping, the General Secretary of the Communist Party, keen to persuade the Dalai Lama to return to Tibet, allowed him to send envoys of his choosing to report on the situation there.

When the separate delegations, led by the Dalai Lama's brother Lobsang Samten and his sister Pema Gyalpo, arrived in 1980, they were mobbed by uncontrollable crowds of devotees who wanted to pay homage to their spiritual leader. Prayer wheels and *khatas*, which had lain hidden for 30 years, were produced in abundance in an overwhelming expression of faith.

The Chinese authorities were horrified; all their attempts to eradicate religion by persecution and indoctrination had been for nought.

Similarly, there was a miraculous and almost instantaneous re-emergence of Buddhism in Mongolia when it was released from the Soviet State in 1990.

Just as the might of America was impotent to counter the regime of Ayatollah Khomeini in Iran, China has found religious unity in Tibet a hard nut to crack.

However Tibetans are not religious fanatics; theirs is a more benign spiritual devotion, which they have never tried to impose on others. Such passionate faith is, nevertheless, a more effective counter to authority than overt political revolt. There is a Tibetan proverb: *Nang-la dra ma-shuna, chi-ki tonta droki mare*, which means: If there is no unity within, nothing can be achieved outside.

Now aware of the strength of Tibetans' feelings, the Chinese realised that the best means to achieve their aims, without incurring dissent amongst the population, was not to outlaw their religion altogether but to control it through indoctrination of the senior lamas. However they implemented this strategy without subtlety and by taking a hard-line, clumsy approach have merely driven the objects for their manipulation into exile.

On 28 December 1999, Urgyen Trinley, the leader of the Kamtsang sub-sect of the Kagyud tradition, fled from the Tshurphu monastery, and made his way to Nepal across the mountains. Having been groomed as a 'patriotic figure', the consequence of the Karmapa Lama's escape was a considerable loss of face for China.

All the other leaders of Tibetan Buddhist sects, the Nyingma, Sakya and Gelug, already reside in India, and China's only remaining card is now the discredited Puppet Panchen – Gyantsen Norbu. There is a joke in Lhasa that "the Karmapa killed Chen Kuiyuan" implying that the recent replacement of the Communist Party Secretary was a consequence of this political embarrassment.

However, a less happy outcome of the incident is that the Kagyud lamas who remain in Tibet have become a target for reprisals. The most important of these is the eight-year-old Pawo *Rinpoche* who has been expelled from his Nyenang monastery near Tshurphu, and forced to attend an ordinary primary school in Lhasa under strict security.

China's illogical behaviour towards the devout, which is so damaging to its aspirations in the modern world, stems from a deep-rooted fear of any spiritual organisation. Religious movements in China have a history of getting out of hand, and the downfall of the Qing Central Government following the upsurge of Buddhist extremism (the Boxers) in 1900 has not been forgotten. Hence the Chinese authorities see all religion as a political problem and its institutions as potential centres of rebellion.

Nevertheless religious groups in China today are undergoing resurgence. There are Christians; Buddhists, particularly in Inner Mongolia as a result of *cho-yon*; and Muslim Uighurs in Xinjiang. All are persecuted. But the most worrying for the Government is the birth of a new religion, which has permeated all levels of Chinese society.

Founded in 1992 by Li Hongzhi, the Falun Gong sect combines Buddhist doctrines with Daoist breathing exercises and encourages a virtuous and peaceful existence. However, unlike other religions, which have a recognised establishment that the authorities can control, the church of the Falun Gong is the Internet and the mobile telephone.

In 1999 10,000 followers surrounded the Zhonguanhai, the seat of Communist power in Beijing, and the shock of this unexpected event spurred a major crackdown throughout China. The Falun Gong was declared an illegal 'heretical cult', and thousands of its practitioners were imprisoned. More arrests and torture followed a repeat demonstration in April 2000 and, in January 2001, five Falun Gong set fire to themselves in Tiananmen Square. Fourteen women died from either suicide or torture in a labour camp in May, and more than 120 followers have been killed by the security forces since July 1999.

A web of falsehoods conceals the wickedness of the PRC's actions as an occupying power in Tibet. Typical of this is the misleading interpretation of Chinese influence upon Tibetan affairs presented to visitors to the Qianlong exhibition in the Lama Temple (Yonghe Gong), Beijing.

Here, amongst the impressive array of treasures, the majority of which have been looted from Tibet, one is told of the Emperor's role in reforming Tibetan Buddhism from immorality and corruption and the creation of the Dalai Lama.

The accompanying English language guidebook does contradict the museum version a little by admitting the part played by the Mongol Khans but then incessantly claims that appointments to the office of Dalai or Panchen Lama could only be made with the permission of the Central Government of the Qing dynasty. It omits any reference to the Chinese invasion of Tibet or the Cultural Revolution.

Unaware of the true state of affairs in Tibet or the historical background to the situation there, the Chinese public believe Tibetans to be an inferior, backward ethnic minority whom the PRC has liberated from serfdom. Their strong feelings against the west and America in particular, were demonstrated by their display of anger following the bombing of the Chinese embassy in Belgrade in 1999, and any criticism of the PRC's behaviour towards religious groups is rebutted with accusations of hypocrisy.

On 1 August 2000, the *China Daily* described the brutality of the Federal Bureau of Investigation towards the Davidians. The US Government has recently been cleared of any wrong-doing during the siege of the cult's compound in Texas in 1993, and the article asks how the US can oppose the David Koresh cult while giving support to the 'evil organisation' of the Falun Gong. Similarly, they cite the 1972 'Bloody Sunday' incident in Londonderry as an example of British religious repression.

The Chinese Vice President Hu Jintao is tipped to succeed the premiership. He was the official responsible for imposing martial law in Lhasa in 1989, and has called for a crackdown on separatism and 'illegal' religious activities in Tibet. There can therefore be little optimism that the Chinese Communist Party will change its policy towards religion in the short term.

However, the younger, better-informed generation

of Chinese will, in time, rise to positions of authority. This, in turn, should lead to political reform. Under a more open and less fearful regime, the coexistence of unfettered religious following within a modern Chinese society might become possible.

The on-going abuse of Tibetan human rights

The Tibetan Centre for Human Rights and Democracy (TCHRD) issued a report for the 2001 World Conference on Racism, which was held in Durban in September. It asserts that the PRC has incorporated ancient racial prejudices in order to serve its contemporary goal of 'Motherland uniformity'.

Justifying itself through the rhetoric of Han superiority, China has attempted to overcome Tibetan identity through derogatory propaganda, economic pressures, and sheer force of numbers. Like the decline of the *kyang* (wild asses) and the black-necked cranes that inhabit this mysterious land, Tibet's unique indigenous population is slowly being eroded to extinction.

Today, much of the horror of the Cultural Revolution lives on. However, through the control of education and health, the destruction of Tibet's distinctive race and heritage, it is conducted more patiently.

Prior to 1950, the nobles provided a source of secular education by holding schools within their households to teach the children of their servants alongside their own. With their demise the opportunity for education in rural areas is now minimal.

In the schools that do exist only Chinese is spoken and the pupils are indoctrinated with Han customs and history. The high fees that are applied to Tibetans prevent two-thirds of the child population from attending school at all and the new minimum age policy for the monasteries has closed off a significant avenue for a traditional Tibetan education. Illiteracy amongst Tibetans has now reached 75 per cent.

Those parents who send their children to schools in India face serious reprisals including suspension from work and cancellation of the child's residence card.

In Tibet, with its dry dusty air, lung diseases are endemic but health care is also discriminatory, the best being only available to the Chinese or the wealthy. Hospitals require a deposit of 1,000 Yuan (£85) before treatment can begin, which is well beyond the means of most Tibetans.

In rural and outlying areas, people resort to traditional spiritual and herbal remedies, or application of the cure-all, yak butter, rather than trust themselves to Chinese 'doctors', who do not have to qualify before practising on Tibetans. As a result, the average life expectancy is a mere 40 years.

There is still enforced sterilisation for women, who are rounded up by armed guards to undergo surgery in makeshift tents set up in the village squares. Those that resist are charged with 'opposing socialism'. Chinese doctors, who receive bonuses for controlling the Tibetan birth rate, are reported to put babies 'to sleep' by injecting alcohol into their brains. The Tibetan infant mortality rate, at 15 per cent, is the highest in the world.

Already, through a process of population transfer from China, 7.5 million Han Chinese now outnumber the meagre, and reducing, population of six million Tibetans. Lhasa plays a key role in Beijing's Western Development programme, and there are plans to quadruple the population by 2005.

Here the Chinese immigrants who benefit from economic favouritism already outnumber their hosts by at least two to one, and the quarter to which the poverty stricken Tibetans are confined comprises less than five per cent of the city. 'The Place of the Gods', where once smoking, mah-jong and even football were banned, is now a den of vice, the revenues from gambling, prostitution and alcohol providing a welcome boost to government coffers. With no urban planning, little traffic control and inadequate sanitation this great jewel of the early explorers is now sinking into a sordid chaos.

The PRC maintains a force of over 300,000 PLA troops in Tibet to keep control, and the treatment of those who resist the authorities remains as brutal as ever. A network of informers makes it dangerous for a Tibetan to speak out against Chinese occupation and there is a hotline number to report anyone suspected of 'unpatriotic activity'.

At present (March 2002) there are 670 Tibetan political prisoners, including 25 children, in captivity. Over 100 Tibetans have died from torture received in jail in the last ten years. The most infamous establishment is the Drapchi Prison, which alone holds 129 captives whose only crime has been to voice dissent. Here, in 1998, guards killed eight inmates for staging a protest.

Naturally, the Chinese have taken steps to ensure that visitors to Tibet do not learn of the true state of affairs. Tourists are presented with a stage-set of selectively restored historic sites that hide the reality of destruction and misery. The apparent well being of the predominantly Chinese population in Lhasa is more *dzuma* - the poverty and suffering of the majority of Tibetans may not be witnessed.

Following the establishment of the Guide Discipline Management Department, 69 Tibetan guides who had been educated in India were sacked in 1999. A further 29 were dismissed from the Shigatse Prefecture Tourist Travel Agency in 2001. Now only those with suitable

The infamous Drapchi prison, Lhasa

indoctrination may have access to foreigners and they are not allowed to discuss the political situation in Tibet or the general condition of the Tibetan people.

The inhabitants of Tibet, in their turn, are denied access to the outside world by control of the media. This includes jamming of international radio broadcasts in an attempt to prevent 'infiltration' of the airwaves by 'foreign hostile forces'. Voice of America, Radio Free Asia and Voice of Tibet, which cover news of the activities of the Dalai Lama and the Tibetan community in exile, all experienced intensified interference with their broadcasts in late 2001.

In September 2000, Guo Jinlong, who comes from Nanjing, took over as Communist Party Secretary of the TAR. In his first major speech he pledged to continue Kuiyuan's policies on the 'struggle against splittism', with the usual disparaging remarks about the Dalai Lama and quoted at length the views of Jiang Zemin and Lenin on the dangers of Western ideological infiltration. Such political speeches are primarily for Beijing's ears, but his declared intention to focus upon economic development in Tibet gives further grounds for concern.

Tibet's environment has already been gravely damaged by deforestation, and China's new policies to industrialise the country with a gas pipe line and improved communication will speed up the decline. The proposed railway from Lhasa to Golmud in Qinghai will facilitate a vast influx of migrant workers, and allow China to rob Tibet of its natural resources with greater efficiency. One thing is certain: only the Chinese and not the Tibetan people will gain benefit from these technological advances.

Tibetans are an intelligent, peaceful race with an inherent compassion for all God's creatures. They are bewildered by the cruelty meted out against them and, strengthened by their faith, the majority wait patiently for better times. In the short term, however, the only way to protect the next generation is to get them out of Tibet and the exodus has trebled recently in light of the worsening situation.

Reception centres in India and Nepal were flooded with over 1,500 refugees under the age of 13 in the first four months of 2001, giving clear evidence of Tibetan's distrust of Chinese promises to educate and employ their children.

There is a proverb that states China's fortune will be dependent upon its treatment of Tibet. It stems from the coincidental collapse of the Qing dynasty with the Chinese invasion of Tibet in 1910, but it retains an element of validity today. China cannot progress without convincing the world of its intention to curb its human rights violations.

No longer can its monstrous behaviour in Tibet be kept secret and, without improvement, the PRC will be denied the international advantages it seeks. China's successful bid to host the 2008 Olympic games places it in the limelight and it will have to watch its step if it is avoid the humiliation of a boycott similar to that experienced by Moscow in 1980.

8

Sovereignty and diplomacy

The Chinese name for Tibet, *Xizang* ('Western Treasure House'), is an indication of its desirability in their eyes. Today it provides them with a wealth of mineral resources, the space to ease their over-population and somewhere to dump their nuclear waste. They will go to great lengths to misrepresent historical facts in order to justify their claim upon it.

China argues that its right to Tibet originated in the 7th century with the marriage of the Chinese Princess Wen Cheng to Songtsen Gampo. They reckon the Mongol Yuan dynasty to be their own and, by association, claim authority over Tibet. In fact, Tibet's spiritual relationship with the Mongol Khans was established some years before the annexation of China in 1279.

The Chinese assume that they inherited the right to rule Tibet when the Ming replaced the Yuan dynasty in

1368 but Tibet had broken off its political relationship with the Mongols in 1350.

While Tibet maintained a strong religious alliance with the Mongol Khans, it had little contact with China during the Ming dynasty. It was not until the Manchu rulers, a distinct Asian Buddhist people, expanded their empire to include China in 1639 that *cho-yon* was re-established with Peking. But Tibetans insist that *cho-yon* was a guarantee by the Emperor to safeguard the person of the Dalai Lama only and not authority to interfere in Tibetan internal affairs. The Chinese dispute this interpretation on account of the demands made by Emperor Qianlong in 1792.

In reality, both sides tend to present somewhat biased versions of their own histories. There was a precedent for high-ranking lamas to seek assistance from China when it suited them but influence in Tibet was not the exclusive right of the Chinese.

At the beginning of the 20th century, Tibet was not a unified nation-state in the European understanding. Despite centralising structures, it included a variety of political and administrative formations, in which a single central power did not consistently maintain authority. Tibet included enclaves under the jurisdiction of Bhutan and Sikkim and, at various times in its history, power centres such as Tashilhunpo conducted dealings with foreign governments without reference to Lhasa.

While there is no doubt that the Manchu rulers did have a large degree of political control over some of Tibet, particularly, in the 18th century, this situation ended with the expulsion of the Chinese from Tibet in 1912 and is no basis for a claim upon Tibetan territory today.

Tibetans believe that all former rights over Tibet, by any power, became superfluous when the 13th Dalai Lama declared independence. This was ratified by formal treaties with Nepal and Mongolia.

In 1960, the International Commission of Jurists' Legal Enquiry Committee in Geneva reported its conclusion that, between 1913 and 1950, Tibet had demonstrated the conditions of statehood recognised by international law.

But Tibetan sovereignty prior to annexation by the Chinese in 1950 is not universally endorsed. In 1943, Sir Anthony Eden stated that Tibet had enjoyed *de facto* independence since 1913, but he is the only British politician to have done so.

Until 1990, British policy had been to recognise China's 'suzerainty'. Since then successive British Governments have reiterated the vague statement that they *"... regard Tibet as autonomous while recognising the special position of the Chinese there."* The Foreign Office Minister, Derek Fatchett, repeated these words to the House of Commons in April 1998, and stated that the British Government did not recognise the Dalai Lama's Government in Exile.

In his 'Five Point Peace Plan', which the Dalai Lama presented to the US Congress in 1987, and to the European Union at Strasbourg in 1988, he proposed that Tibet should become a 'Zone of Peace', in which fundamental human rights and democratic freedoms should be restored, population control and environmental damage halted and the foundations established for negotiation on the future status of Tibet.

This proposal was withdrawn in 1991 but, in a speech given in Poland in May 2000, the Dalai Lama explained that he did not seek independence but a *"genuine autonomy within the framework of the PRC"* - whereby Tibetans would have control over their internal affairs under the umbrella of China for defence and foreign policy.

Such devolution from China, which the Dalai Lama now calls his 'Middle Way Approach', is similar to the arrangements proposed by the British at the Simla Convention in 1914. In October 2001 the Dalai Lama addressed the European Parliament to seek their support. Here he reaffirmed his commitment to a peaceful solution but pressed China to enter into a dialogue on the matter.

In 1990, the *Kashag* and parliament in Dharamsala became fully democratic having been elected by the 134,000 Tibetans living in exile. On 29 July 2001 they elected their *Kalon Tripa* (Prime Minister) for the first time.

The Dalai Lama has said that, if he is returned to Tibet, he will stand down as its political leader once a democratically elected government had been established in Lhasa. In 1989 he was awarded the Nobel Peace Prize for his non-violent struggle to achieve more freedom for the Tibetan people.

The Dalai Lama receiving the 1989 Nobel Peace Prize

The Chinese have an intense sensitivity over issues of territorial integrity, which applies equally to Hong Kong, Macao and Taiwan; the dilemma is that they do not trust the Dalai Lama not to seek full independence and 'split the Motherland' once he has a foot in the door.

In 1993, they severed all formal channels of communication with Dharamsala and, in 1998, during a joint Press conference with President Clinton in Beijing, Jiang Zemin stated that he would not restore negotiations until the Dalai Lama recognised that both Tibet and Taiwan were inalienable parts of China.

During August 2000, Gyalo Thondup, another of the Dalai Lama's brothers, with a view to opening up dialogue, held talks with Chinese Consular officials in Beijing. However, the Chinese Foreign Ministry spokeswoman, Zhang Qiyue, claimed that he was only there in a personal capacity rather than as a representative of the Tibetan Government in Exile. She reiterated the usual line that the Dalai Lama must state that Tibet is part of China and *"cease his splittist activities"* and said that Beijing had not seen any sincerity from the Dalai Lama's side regarding possible talks.

International response

After the Gulf War the Dalai Lama asked: *"Why help Kuwait and not Tibet? The atrocities conducted in Kuwait lasted a few months. What the Chinese have done to Tibet has lasted for 45 years!"* No doubt he must have had similar sentiments after the Kosovo crisis.

In truth, the West has been weak in its support for Tibet, but there are reasons for this. In 1950, Britain had recently withdrawn from India and the Allies were averse to confronting the Chinese, who had faced a common enemy during the Second World War. When Mao Tse-tung began to renege on the 'Seventeen Point Agreement', the West was preoccupied with the Korean War and reluctant to expand conflict in the Far East.

Later, the Cold War and Vietnam each became a focus of attention. It is unfortunate for Tibet that, despite international concern for her plight, direct involvement was thwarted by more pressing issues. However, reluctance to assist Tibet during that early period was influenced strongly by her unimpressive record of self-government prior to 1950.

With its mare's nest of domestic politics, the exasperating nature of Tibet's shifting allegiances and religious power struggles made her an unreliable ally, for whom overt support posed some risk. But, critically, the Tibetan Government had failed to formalise its independence in the 1920s by establishing diplomatic representation abroad. Tibet's insistence upon isolation from the world denied her a voice in the International Community so, when the Chinese invaded, her tardy cry for help went unheard.

There is now a political environment more suitable for condemnation of the PRC's treatment of Tibetans, but all attempts at censure have to date been ineffective. The General Assembly of the United Nations adopted resolutions on Tibet in 1959, 1961 and 1965, but, faced with China's veto in the Security Council, it is powerless to act. UNSCR 1723 called for *"... the cessation of practices which deprive the Tibetan people of their fundamental rights and freedoms, including the right to self-determination"*.

But the legality of interference on humanitarian grounds by States or alliances in the internal affairs of another is a key issue applicable to NATO's intervention in Kosovo and Russia's in Chechnaya. Russia therefore supports China in the Security Council over its resistance to outside involvement.

Indeed, since the tragic event of September 11, 2001 in New York, Russia and China may demand impunity from censure of their own conduct as the price for acquiescence with the West's campaign against international terrorism.

However, the United States Congress, particularly under the Republicans, has been an exponent of support for Tibet. It became one of the few parliaments to recognise Tibet's true status when, in October 1991, President George Bush (senior) signed into law a Congressional Resolution declaring Tibet an occupied country.

The US also provides a 'Special Envoy for Tibet' with the rank of ambassador, to promote good relations with the Tibetan Government in Exile. In January 2000, Congress tabled an 81-page draft resolution at the UN High Commission for Human Rights, but, as a result of lack-lustre lobbying, exemplified by President Clinton's silence on the matter, it failed.

China countered with a no-action motion that was supported by Bangladesh, Bhutan, India, and Pakistan - all countries that fear confrontation with a powerful neighbour. The motion was passed by four votes and following endorsement by the Commission in April the Chinese have now secured immunity from investigation for the time being.

China's 14-year quest to be accepted by the World Trade Organisation (WTO) provided an avenue for the US and the EU to apply leverage on human rights issues which is now lost. On 24 May 2000, the US House of Representatives voted to grant Beijing Permanent Normal Trade Relations, which, as one of the terms for

Sovereignty and diplomacy

WTO accession, paved the way for approval by the Senate in June. An agreement between the EU and Beijing on trade removed the final obstacle and China became a member of the WTO later in the year.

Trade is a stronger driver of policy than human rights. Nepal has reviewed its 1950 Border Treaty Agreement in a move to improve relations with China and gain economic favours. Tighter controls now make it more difficult for Tibetans to escape and early in 2001 Nepalese border guards shot dead two Tibetan monks as they tried to cross the frontier.

However, the massacre of the Royal Family in June 2001 is likely to have more far-reaching consequences. The volatile political balance in Nepal had been held in check by a strong and revered monarch in King Birendra. But distrust of the new king, Gyanandra and, particularly his unpopular son, Crown Prince Paras, a drug-abusing playboy who was responsible for the death of a pop idol, may turn Nepalis away from loyalty to the Crown.

Maoist insurgents have become increasingly active in Nepal, killing 60 policemen in 2001 alone and a rise in support for the movement could lead to all out revolt. This would play into China's hands and create further instability in the Himalayas.

Britain was the only western country ever to have treaty relations with Tibet but, despite its earlier influence in the region, absolved itself from responsibility when it withdrew from India in 1947, and sold the Tibetans down the river. Although it claimed to support the policies of the Indian Government, under

Nehru, during discussions on Tibet's status in the United Nations in 1950, Britain has exercised a somewhat lubricious policy on the issue ever since.

After the atrocities of 1959, the British Government even declined to support a resolution in the UN condemning the violation of human rights in Tibet by the Chinese. Hugh Richardson, the last Head of Mission in Lhasa, who had been charged with passing to the Tibetans assurances of British support, felt bitterly betrayed.

More recently, Britain was one of the few countries

Hugh Richardson, the last Head of Mission in Lhasa, felt bitterly betrayed by the British government

not to issue a formal protest at the abduction of Choekyi Nyima. In 2000, during the annual UN Conference on Human Rights in Geneva, the US expressed dismay at the UK's lack of positive support for its attempts to censure China.

There has been some excuse for Britain's silence in the past. The British invasion of Tibet by Colonel Younghusband's force in 1903 could provoke an accusation of hypocrisy, and, at the time of the latest Panchen Lama controversy, the Government was preoccupied with the transfer of Hong Kong and unwilling to jeopardise negotiations by causing offence.

The All Party Parliamentary Group for Tibet monitors developments closely and one of its members, the Earl of Carrick, led a motion on Tibet in the House of Lords in May 1999, coinciding with a visit to London by the Dalai Lama. Despite this, there was no official contact with the Dalai Lama by a representative of the government.

Although claiming to place human rights at the heart of its foreign policy, this present Labour government has been particularly unctuous towards China. This was clearly demonstrated by the measures taken to spare Jiang Zemin from embarrassment during his state visit to London in October 1999. The heavy-handed policing of that event was later declared unlawful by an independent inquiry.

Supporters of Tibet distrust the Government's preference for isolated 'constructive dialogue' rather than supporting international censure and blame the deterioration of conditions in Tibet on this pusillanimous approach.

The stark reality is that, faced with a huge new market and lucrative contracts, the West chooses to place exploitation of the world's seventh largest and fastest growing economy above concern for its deplorable human rights record and behaviour towards minority peoples within the PRC.

The lamentable omission of the Dalai Lama, a Nobel Peace Laureate, from the UN Millennium Peace Summit for over 1,000 world religious delegates that was held in August 2001 is a case in point. Such fear of causing offence and the absence of effective formal censure only serves to encourage China, and allows the continuing evasion of interference in its internal affairs without much hindrance.

9

བོད་རང་བཙན།

Conclusion

Tibet is an ancient Buddhist civilisation. The Mongol Emperors encouraged the ascendancy of Tibet's religious teachers and, in the 17th century, the most powerful of these, the Dalai Lama, became head of state. Henceforth the lineage of Tibet's celibate leaders has been determined by reincarnation and a relationship was formed between the Dalai Lama and the second senior hierarch, the Panchen Lama, that established the precedent for mutual recognition of each other's reborn heir.

During the Qing dynasty, the Buddhist Manchu conquerors of China assumed responsibility for the Dalai Lama's protection in exchange for spiritual patronage, but this led to demands for greater control over Tibetan affairs, including the selection of high-ranking lamas. However, Manchu influence diminished at the end of the 19th century, and in 1913 Tibet declared itself independent.

Conclusion

Modern China draws selectively upon history to justify its territorial claims and exploits Tibet's religious tradition for its own political ends. In particular, it has capitalised on the linkage between the two leading lamas. Both the Imperialist and Nationalist Chinese tried to use the Ninth Panchen Lama to exert pressure upon the Dalai Lama and when they occupied Amdo in 1949, the Communists were able to abduct and indoctrinate the Tenth.

Unsuccessful in their efforts to undermine the influence of the Dalai Lama since 1959, the PRC Government believe his hold over the Tibetan people from exile in Dharamsala poses a significant challenge to their authority. Thus, when the Tenth Panchen Lama died in 1989, the Chinese were determined to maintain control of the office that could sanction their choice of Tibet's spiritual leader in the future.

The search for the reincarnation of the latest Panchen Lama was therefore a political issue and, when the Dalai Lama usurped the PRC's authority by announcing the appointment of Choekyi Nyima in 1995, he triggered a brutal campaign against Tibetan nationalism and an upsurge in religious repression. In order to restore their ability to manipulate religious affairs, the Chinese imprisoned the Tibetan choice of Panchen and replaced him with an impostor. The 12-year-old lama and his family have not been seen since 1995, and there is now some concern that Choekyi Nyima might be dead.

Tibetans are fundamentally religious. Their country

and their faith are inextricably linked in their thoughts. But, while they may be dominated by medieval superstitions, and can be obstinate and secretive in their dealings with *chilingpa* (strangers), they are an intelligent and devout people who have an inherent regard for the truth. They are incurably cheerful and, with their love of humour and song, they have a character that bears no resemblance to that of their captors.

By contrast, the Chinese, who have traditionally seen their own ancient culture as a reason to treat foreigners with haughty disdain, have no scruples in misrepresenting history for political or any other purpose. What Chinese theory decrees is to them reality, regardless of truth, and flights of imagination are easily ingrained in the minds of subjects in an authoritarian State.

Despite any recent political indoctrination, the Chinese retain a mystic reverence for the past. This leads them to cling to their historic influence over any territory that once formed part of their dominions, and to believe that former allies still desire that unity, whatever the appearances may be.

Hence, the present Chinese regime claims that Tibet is an inalienable part of China. They believe that traits of national identity contradict communist ideology and threaten their territorial integrity. As a result, Tibet's language and culture are being eradicated by indoctrination and its people ethnically cleansed by population transfer and systematic racism.

Conclusion

The Communists fear religion in general and the Dalai Lama's spiritual influence in particular. Religious persecution has recently been increased but Tibet is a sacred land, and the devotion of its people to the Buddhist faith cannot be demolished easily.

By exploiting the traditional relationship between Tibet's two leading hierarchs, the Chinese see control of the Panchen Lamas as a means to divide loyalties and thus weaken religious authority. Ultimately, they wish to ensure that the reincarnation of Tenzin Gyatso is their own man.

The treatment of Gedhun Choekyi Nyima is just one more tragedy in the catalogue of atrocity committed in Tibet. But the contortions that were necessary to control the latest Panchen Lama's appointment, and the brutality of its aftermath, serve to illustrate the extent of Beijing's extraordinary paranoia.

At the beginning of the 20th century, the behaviour of the British, in the aftermath of their expedition to Lhasa, was remembered with approval by Tibetans. The treatment of the 13th Dalai Lama while in exile in India (1910-1912) established a strong bond of friendship between Britain and Tibet.

More than 100 British-Indian officials and their supporting staffs lived and worked in Tibet between 1904 and 1947. They secured the trust of the Tibetan people and earned for the Raj a privileged position of influence in the region. But when the British withdrew from India in 1947, they essentially washed their hands of Tibet.

Conclusion

It was Tibet's misfortune that, having been released from the influence of a fundamentally benign imperial power, she was promptly conquered by a ruthless and barbaric dictatorship, whose exploitation and oppression of Tibet and its people still continues.

Outwardly Tibetans still smile but inside they have been crying for 50 years. No individual nation has been treated as badly as Tibet and, in part, this Himalayan tragedy must lie on British conscience. A more robust and multi-lateral approach by the international community is now needed to persuade the PRC to respect human rights, restore relations with the Dalai Lama and provide evidence of Gedhun Choekyi Nyima's well being. Britain has a moral responsibility to take a more proactive role in this endeavour.

To allow the current policy of persecution by China to continue is to risk revolt by the Tibetan people in the future. Tenzin Gyatso's ceaseless quest for a non-violent solution to resolve the issue of Tibet's autonomy provides the best hope for peace in the region. This is a dark time for the 'Land of Snows' and the phrase "Long live the Dalai Lama" has never been so poignant.

Appendix 1

The control of Tibet prior to the Dalai Lamas

The emperors of Tibet (Tsanpo)

7th   (641) Marriage of Songtsen Gampo to the Tang and Nepalese princesses – introduction to Buddhism.

8th   (763) Conquest of China.
Nyingma Sect founded by Padmasambhava – establishment of Buddhism.

9th   Assassination of Ralpa-chan and the destruction of Buddhism.
Death of Langdarma ends dynasty of the Tsanpo.

The rule of the warlords

10th   Tibet's provinces ruled by warlords for the next 200 years.

11th   Sakya sect founded by Khon Konchok Gyalpo.
Kagyud sect founded by Marpa.

Tibet under the Sakya Lamas

13th   (1239) Invasion of Tibet by Prince Godan.
Cho-yon established between Sakya lamas and Mongolia.
Kunga Gyaltsen's alliance with Godan Khan.
Drogon Choegyal Phagpa's alliance with Kublai Khan.
(1271) Mongol Yuan dynasty replaces Chinese Sung dynasty.

The Tibetan Sitya Dynasty

14th   (1350) The Tibetan king Changchub Gyaltsen breaks off relations with Mongolia and removes the Sakya lamas from power.
(1368) Chinese Ming dynasty formed.

Appendix 1

15th   Gelug sect founded by Je Tsongkhapa.

16th   (1578) Head of the Gelugpa sect given the title "Dalai Lama" by Altan Khan.

The Kings of Tsang and The Karmapa Lama

17th   (1605) Karmapa Lama installed by Tsangba Khan – end of the Sitya dynasty.

(1640) Fifth Dalai Lama installed as spiritual and temporal leader of Tibet by Gushri Khan.

The Dalai Lamas

Appendix 2

The Dalai and Panchen lineages

Tsongkhapa
(Lobsang Drakpa – born in Amdo 1357)

Dalai Lamas	Panchen Lamas
1391- *1st* Gendun Drub **1475** *Nephew of Tsongkhapa* *Founded Tashilhunpo*	**1385-** *1st* Khedrup Gelek Pelsang **1438**
	1439- *2nd* Sonam Choklang **1504**
1470- *2nd* Gyalwa Gendun **1542** Gyatso *Son of a Mongolian prince -* *First reincarnation*	**1505-** *3rd* Wensa Lobsang **1564** Dondrub
1543- 3rd Gyalwa Sonam **1588 Gyatso** *Created **Dalai** Lama by* *Altan Khan in 1578 His two* *predecessors were given the* *title retrospectively*	
	1570- 4th Lobsang Choekyi **1662 Gyaltsen** *Forced the king of Tsang to* *allow the search for the Fifth* *Dalai Lama* *Created **Panchen** Lama by* *Ngawang Lobsang Gyatso for* *his role as tutor and given* *control of Tashilhunpo* *monastery. His three* *predecessors were given the title* *retrospectively*
1589- 4th Yonten Gyatso **1617** *Murdered by Tsangba Khan*	

Appendix 2

Dalai Lamas	**Panchen Lamas**

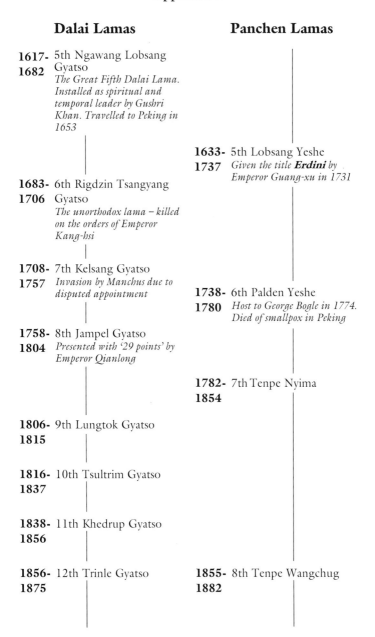

**1617-
1682** 5th Ngawang Lobsang Gyatso
The Great Fifth Dalai Lama. Installed as spiritual and temporal leader by Gushri Khan. Travelled to Peking in 1653

**1633-
1737** 5th Lobsang Yeshe
*Given the title **Erdini** by Emperor Guang-xu in 1731*

**1683-
1706** 6th Rigdzin Tsangyang Gyatso
The unorthodox lama – killed on the orders of Emperor Kang-hsi

**1708-
1757** 7th Kelsang Gyatso
Invasion by Manchus due to disputed appointment

**1738-
1780** 6th Palden Yeshe
Host to George Bogle in 1774. Died of smallpox in Peking

**1758-
1804** 8th Jampel Gyatso
Presented with '29 points' by Emperor Qianlong

**1782-
1854** 7th Tenpe Nyima

**1806-
1815** 9th Lungtok Gyatso

**1816-
1837** 10th Tsultrim Gyatso

**1838-
1856** 11th Khedrup Gyatso

**1856-
1875** 12th Trinle Gyatso

**1855-
1882** 8th Tenpe Wangchug

Appendix 2

Dalai Lamas

1876- 13th Thubten Gyatso
1933 *Exiled in Mongolia during British invasion in 1904, and in India during Chinese invasion in 1910. Declared Tibet independent in 1913. Dispute with Panchen Lama*

1935- 14th Tenzin Gyatso
Ruler of Tibet at time of Chinese invasion in 1950. Exiled in India since 1959. Nobel Peace Prize laureate and champion for the cause of Tibetan people. Recognised Gedhun Choekyi Nyima in 1995

Panchen Lamas

1883- 9th Choe-ki Nyima
1937 *Visited India in 1905. Usurped Dalai Lama and went into exile in 1923*

1938- 10th Choekyi Gyaltsen
1989 *Cultivated by the PRC but imprisoned in China 1962-1977. Died at Tashilhunpo in suspicious circumstances*

1989- 11th Gedhun Choekyi Nyima
Abducted by the Chinese immediately after his recognition in 1995. Whereabouts unknown

Appendix 3

The Tibet Cadre

Colonel Sir Francis Younghusband
Mission to Lhasa (1903-1904)

Lt. Colonel Sir Frank O'Connor
Trade Agent Gyantse (1904-1907)

Major Eric Bailey
Trade Agent Gyantse (1907-1909)
Political Officer of Sikkim (1921-1928)

Claude White
Political Officer of Sikkim (1889-1908)

David Macdonald
Trade Agent Yatung (1911-1918)

Sir Charles Bell
Political Officer of Sikkim (1904-1920)

Frank Ludlow
Headmaster Gyantse School (1923-1926)

Lt. Colonel James Weir
Trade Agent Gyantse (1909-1911)
Political Officer of Sikkim (1928-1933)

Frederick Williamson
Trade Agent Gyantse (1924-1926)
Political Officer of Sikkim (1926-1935)

Sir Basil Gould
Political Officer of Sikkim (1914-1945)

Hugh Richardson
Head of Mission in Lhasa (1937-1950)

Notes:

1. A large number of officials served in Tibet on behalf of the British Raj in the first half of the twentieth century. Only those mentioned in the text are listed here.

2. The Political Officers Sikkim held office in Gantok at various times between the dates shown.

3. F M "Eric" Bailey is also renowned in horticultural circles for discovering the Blue Poppy – *Meconopsis baileyi*.

4. Hugh Richardson remained in Lhasa to head the mission on behalf of the Indian Government from 1947-1950. (He was the founding member of the Tibet Society of UK and died on 2 December 2000)

Appendix 4

Glossary

Amban	representative of the Manchu emperors, a position created in 1727 and abolished by the 13th Dalai Lama in 1913.
Bodhisattva	the highest level of reincarnation - a being who has renounced his own final liberation to deliver all living creatures into enlightenment.
Bon	the original Tibetan religion.
Cham	dances performed during religious ceremonies
Chang	Tibetan beer.
Chenrezig	The *Bodhisattva* of perfect compassion (skt: Avolokitesvara).
Chida	Commander General of the Tibetan Army.
Chikyab Khenpo	Lord Chamberlain.
Chilingpa	foreigners.
Chingtro	Chinese "liberation" of Tibet.
Chipa	non-Buddhist "outsider".
Chomolungma	Mount Everest.
Chorten	*Stupa* or shrine
Cho-yon	a term combining two words *choney* ("that which is worthy of veneration") and *yondag* ("he who gives offerings"). Also known as *yon-mchod*. This term referred to the Priest-Patron relationship established between the Emperors and the Tibetan lamas.
Chuba	traditional Tibetan gown.
Chu-shi Gang-druk	Four Rivers, Six Ranges - the traditional collective name for the two provinces of Kham and Amdo)
Dalai(Lama)	"Ocean of Wisdom" from the Mongolian word for ocean. The earthly manifestation of Chenresig, Bodhisattva of Compassion. Referred to by some Tibetans as *Gyal-wa Rinpoche* meaning "Precious Majesty"; *Kundun*

Appendix 4

	"The Presence"; or *Yishi Norbu* "Wish-Granting Jewel".
Dayan	silver dollars.
Depon	General in the Tibetan army.
Dharma	Buddhist teachings – literally "the path".
Dob dob	warrior monk.
Dri	female yak.
Dzong	castle or fort.
Dzuma	all show (Chinese sham).
Erdeni	a title meaning "precious jewel" conferred on the Fifth Panchen Lama by the Manchu Emperor.
Ganden tripa	literally, "the one who sits on the throne of the Ganden Monastery" - the head of the Gelugpa lineage.
Gangs-ljongs	the Tibetan name for Tibet - "land of snows"
Geshe	doctor of Buddhist philosophy in the Gelugpa school.
Gompa	monastery.
Gyangshing	pillory yoke.
Hutuktu	the religious leader of Mongolia.
Inji	Englishmen.
Kalachakra	"The Wheel of Time", a complex yoga tantra and profound Buddhist teaching.
Kalon	minister of the Tibetan government.
Kalon Tripa	Prime Minister
Karma	chain of actions from one life to another.
Kashag	council of ministers composed of three lay *kalons* and one religious *kalon lama*. Members hold the title *Shappe*.
Khata	white silk scarf used as an offering by Tibetans.
Khenpo	administrative council of Tashilhunpo, headed by the Panchen Lama.
Kuden	oracle who acts as a medium between the natural and spiritual realms.
Kuden-la	the State Oracle (La is honorific – i.e. special kuden).

Appendix 4

Kutenla	the state oracle.
Kyang	wild ass unique to Tibet.
... la	Tibetan word for pass.
Ladug	"pass poison" – altitude sickness.
Lama	Tibetan Buddhist teacher.
Laogai	Chinese labour camp –'Reform through labour'.
Lhakhang	chapel – literally 'residence of the god'.
Lhasa	place of the gods.
Lingkhor	pilgrimage circuit.
Losar	celebrations of the Tibetan New Year.
Maitreya	the 'Buddha of the Future', who embodies universal love.
Mandala	a symbolic two- or three-dimensional representation of a deity's realm or exisitence, created in metal, paint or coloured.
Mantra	a syllable of prayer that is uttered repetitively to help a person gain access to the innermost mind. The most common is *Om mani padme hum* - "Hail to the jewel in the Lotus".
Mo	dice divination.
Monlam Chenmo	prayer festival and collective rituals of greeting performed during *Losar*.
Nangmagang	the office of the Panchen Lama.
Nangpa	Buddhist "insider" – Tibetan term for their identity.
Ngak-pa	a tantric practitioner.
Norbu	jewel.
Norbulingka	the "Garden of Jewels" - the Dalai Lama's summer palace.
Palden Lhamo	the female protector of Tibet.
Panchen(Lama)	Great Scholar - composite of the Sanskrit word pandita meaning "scholar" and the Tibetan word chenpo meaning "great". The earthly manifestation of Amithaba ("the Infinite Light") or O-pa-me, a deity that is even more revered than the Dalai Lama's Chenresig. The Panchen Lamas are also sometimes referred to

	as the Tashi Lamas due to their seat at the Tashilhunpo monastery.
Potala	the Dalai Lama's winter palace.
Pundit	native surveyor sent into Tibet by the British Raj.
Rinpoche	literally, "Precious One", an honorary title for lamas with high spiritual realisations.
Shakyamuni	The historical Buddha born in Nepal c. 565 BC.
Shappe	title given to members of the *Kashag*.
Srung mdud	Buddhist protection cords
Stupa	religious monument, often containing relics of former lamas.
Sutra	texts reporting the Buddha's original teachings.
Takril	the practice of rolling dough balls to determine reincarnations.
Taphue	ceremonial shaving of a boy lama's head.
Tashilhunpo	"Magnificent Auspiciousness" – the literal name for the monastery at Shigatse.
Thamzing	'struggle' sessions of public self-criticism implemented by the Chinese communists.
Thangka	a Tibetan scroll painting on cotton or silk.
Trungche	the Dalai Lama's Chief Secretary
Tsampa	roasted barley flour.
Tsang	the ancient province of Tibet west of Lhasa.
Tsanpo	the title of "emperor" conferred on the rulers of Tibet between the 7th and 11th centuries.
Tsenshap	tutor of a *tulku*.
Tsongdu	the National Assembly of the Kashag.
Tulku	a child recognised as the reincarnation of a deceased teacher and installed as the head of his predecessor's institution.
U	the original name for the province of Lhasa.
Xizang	'Western Treasure House' – The Chinese name for Tibet.

Bibliography

Avedon J
In Exile from the Land of Snows, New York: Harper Perennial, 1997

Bell C
Tibet Past & Present, Oxford: Clarendon Press, 1924
The People of Tibet, Oxford: Clarendon Press, 1928
Portrait of the Dalai Lama, London: Collins, 1946

Bishop I
Among the Tibetans, Oxford: Hart, 1894

Chambers J
Genghis Khan, Stroud: Sutton Publishing, 1999

Feigon L
Demystifying Tibet, London: Profile Books, 1999

Fleming P
The Siege at Peking, London: Hart-Davis, 1959
Bayonets to Lhasa, Hong Kong: Oxford University Press, 1961

Ford R
Captured in Tibet, London: Harrap & Co., 1957

French P
Younghusband, London: Harper Collins, 1995

Goldstein M
A History of Modern Tibet, University of California Press, 1989

Guibaut A
Tibetan Venture, London: Murray, 1947

Bibliography

Harrer H
Seven Years in Tibet, London: Harper Collins, 1953
Return to Tibet, London: Weidenfeld & Nicolson, 1984

Hilton I
The Search for the Panchen Lama, London: Penguin Group, 1999

Lamb H
Genghis Khan – Emperor of All Men, London: Butterworth Ltd, 1928

Landon P
Lhasa, London: Hurst & Blacket, 1905

Macdonald D
Twenty Years in Tibet (1904-1924), Delhi: Genesis, reprint 1996

Martin C
The Boxer Rebellion, New York: Abelard-Schuman, 1968

McKay A
Tibet and the British Raj, London: Curzon Press, 1997

Richardson H
High Peaks, Pure Earth, London: Serindia Publications, 1998
Papers, Gantok: Sikkim Research Institute of Tibetology, 1993

Tenzin Gyatso - HH The Dalai Lama
Freedom in Exile, London: Abacus, 1998

Thubten Norbu
Tibet is my Country, London: Hart-Davis, 1960

Tsarong D
In the service of his country, New York: Snow Lion Publications, 2000

Tsering T
The Panchen Lama Lineage, Dharamsala: DIIR, 1996

Van Grasdorff G
Hostage of Beijing, Shaftesbury: Element Books, 1999

Bibliography

Shao-ru C
Yonghe Gong, Beijing: China Publishing House, 1995

Shakya T
The Dragon in the Land of Snows, London: Pimlico, 1999

White J
Twenty-One Years on the North-East Frontier, London: 1909

Articles

Berkin M, *An Ethical Foreign Policy for Tibet*, London: May 2000

Clark P, *Background to British policy on Tibet*, London: FCO, Apr 1995

Hunter A, *A Qing Lottery and Chinese Legitimacy in Tibet*, Leeds: Jan 2000

Kuleshov N, *Tibet Policies of Britain and Russia, 1900-14*, Moscow: Oct 1996

Samphel T, *DIIR Information Sheets, Dharamsala*: Jan 2000

Other sources

The Tibet Society of the United Kingdom (Zara Fleming)
www.tibetsociety.com

The Tibet Information Network
www.tibetinfo.net

The Tibet Government in Exile
www.tibet.com

Index

Index

174

Index

Index